Series/Number 07-103

DATA ANALYSIS
An Introduction

MICHAEL S. LEWIS-BECK
University of Iowa

SAGE PUBLICATIONS
International Educational and Professional Publisher
Thousand Oaks   London   New Delhi

For information address:

SAGE Publications, Inc.
2455 Teller Road
Thousand Oaks, California 91320
E-mail: order@sagepub.com

SAGE Publications Ltd.
6 Bonhill Street
London EC2A 4PU
United Kingdom

SAGE Publications India Pvt. Ltd.
M-32 Market
Greater Kailash I
New Delhi 110 048 India

Printed in the United States of America

Library of Congress Cataloging-in-Publication Data

Lewis-Beck, Michael S.
    Data analysis: an introduction / Michael S. Lewis-Beck.
        p. cm. — (Sage university papers series. Quantitative
    applications in the social sciences; no. 07-103)
    Includes bibliographical references.
    ISBN 0-8039-5772-6 (alk. paper)
    1. Social sciences—Statistical methods   I. Title. II. Series.
HA29.L49   1995
300'.1'5195—dc20   94-45242

    97 98 99 00 10 9 8 7 6 5 4 3

Sage Project Editor: Susan McElroy

When citing a university paper, please use the proper form. Remember to cite the current Sage University Paper series title and include the paper number. One of the following formats can be adapted (depending on the style manual used):

(1) LEWIS-BECK, M. S. (1995) *Data Analysis: An Introduction.* Sage University Paper series on Quantitative Applications in the Social Sciences, 07-103. Thousand Oaks, CA: Sage.

OR

(2) Lewis-Beck, M. S. (1995) *Data analysis: An introduction* (Sage University Paper series on Quantitative Applications in the Social Sciences, 07-103). Thousand Oaks, CA: Sage.

To Frank M. Andrews
Who taught how to put words to numbers

CONTENTS

SERIES EDITOR'S INTRODUCTION

Webster's New Collegiate Dictionary defines "data" (plural of "datum") as a "group of facts." Social science data then are facts—empirical observations—from the world of human behavior. Popular notions to the contrary, facts do not speak for themselves. The task of data analysts is to try to give meaning to the facts. I say "try" to give meaning because if the data are bad, then they will yield no interpretation, or a false one. Assuming that the data are good, then analysis can lead to sensible description or explanation of the social phenomenon under study.

Data analysis involves the systematic application of statistical tools. How do we come to acquire these tools and use them properly? As with the efficient learning of many skills, one begins with the simple parts first, using them as building blocks for more complicated ones. For example, it is a mistake, made often by beginning students, to skip over preliminaries and jump immediately into multiple regression analysis. To appreciate multiple regression, you need initially to acquire a firm foundation in univariate and bivariate statistics. By learning, say, about the correlation coefficient (Pearson's r) between two variables, you familiarize yourself with such concepts as association, strength, linearity, measurement level, inference, and standardization. This provides groundwork for understanding bivariate regression, which is different, but not completely so. Further, once a good handle on bivariate regression is acquired, the extension to multiple regression comes relatively easily, and with more comprehension.

This monograph aims to provide the statistical fundamentals that every data analyst needs in order to launch a quantitative research project. After a brief discussion of data gathering, univariate statistics (measures of central tendency and dispersion) are considered. Then measures of association (Pearson's r, tau, lambda) and significance testing are looked at and, finally, simple and multiple regression are developed. Formulas are provided but their interpretation in plain English is stressed. Also, figures are used whenever they can help tell the story. Throughout, there is much application, based on a unifying example—how to explain academic ability from data on a sample of college students.

Recalling to mind the title of the series—*Quantitative Applications in the Social Sciences*—the current volume could be regarded as a gateway to the others. Further, once it is read, the series itself offers many titles on each of the subjects introduced here. For example, on data gathering see *Introduction to Survey Sampling* (No. 35, Kalton), *Using Published Data* (No. 42, Jacob), *Secondary Analysis of Survey Data* (No. 53, Kiecolt & Nathan), *Survey Questions* (No. 63, Converse & Presser), and *Processing Data* (No. 85, Bourque & Clark); on univariate statistics see *Central Tendency and Variability* (No. 83, Weisberg) and *Nonparametric Statistics* (No. 90, Gibbons); on bivariate statistics see *Analysis of Nominal Data* (No. 7, Reynolds), *Analysis of Ordinal Data* (No. 8, Hildebrand, Laing, & Rosenthal), *Measures of Association* (No. 32, Liebetrau), and *Nonparametric Measures of Association* (No. 91, Gibbons); on significance tests see *Tests of Significance* (No. 4, Henkel) and *Understanding Significance Testing* (No. 73, Mohr); on regression see *Applied Regression* (No. 22, Lewis-Beck), *Multiple Regression in Practice* (No. 50, Berry & Feldman), *Interaction Effects in Multiple Regression* (No. 72, Jaccard, Turrisi, & Wan), *Regression Diagnostics* (No. 79, Fox), *Understanding Regression Assumptions* (No. 92, Berry), and *Regression With Dummy Variables* (No. 93, Hardy).

—*Michael S. Lewis-Beck*
Series Editor

ACKNOWLEDGMENTS

Many have contributed to the development of this monograph. I would like to thank Bill Berry, Helmut Norpoth, and Herb Weisberg, all of the Editorial Board, for extremely useful comments on earlier drafts. Also, I wish to acknowledge my quantitative methods teachers at the University of Michigan, among them Frank M. Andrews, Institute for Social Research, who recently passed away and to whom this volume is dedicated. Additionally, from Michigan, I express a special appreciation to Larry Mohr. As well, I extend thanks to my wife J. Arline Lewis-Beck, Ph.D., who formatted the equations in the text. The graduate students of the University of Iowa deserve recognition, for it is with them that I have tested many previous versions of this material; and the students of the TARKI Summer School in Budapest, who were the first to be exposed to the (almost) final version. Last, I want to thank C. Deborah Laughton, Editor at Sage, who has helped me vastly on this and several other projects.

DATA ANALYSIS
An Introduction

MICHAEL S. LEWIS-BECK
University of Iowa

1. INTRODUCTION

Social science research begins with a question about human behavior. The questions are different, depending on the discipline. Here are some examples. Are women more likely to vote than men? What makes for satisfaction on the job? Does higher unemployment lead to an increase in crime? To improve student performance, should the mode of instruction be discussion rather than lecture? If a community accepts a chemical waste treatment facility, are its citizens at higher risk for cancer? Respectively, these questions would probably be posed in political science, psychology, sociology, education, and health policy. Of course, they could be answered by any quantitative social scientist, with a methodology that unites the seemingly varied disciplines. That is, all rely on systematic empirical observation, followed by the application of statistical tests. These test results—the data analysis—help answer the research question. The better the execution of the analysis, the stronger the conclusions.

Although quantitative researchers may have an interest in the same question and draw on the same set of statistical tools, that does not mean they necessarily utilize precisely the same strategy of inquiry. Some are formal in their approach, laying out detailed hypotheses and measures, then judiciously applying selected final tests. Others are informal, giving free play to the exploration of ideas and data, willingly conducting different estimations in search of the "correct" model. Good researchers know the limits of both these strategies, knowing when to rely on formal procedures and when to trust to a discovery. Judgment must ultimately be exercised in properly interpreting any statistical result, especially when it comes from nonexperimental social research, the focus of this monograph.

Of course, an investigator who demonstrates mastery of technique more surely carries the day in scholarly debate. The intention here is to give the beginning social science researcher a ready ability to select and evaluate statistical tests appropriate for the question at hand. Chapter 2 considers the initial task of data gathering, offering a data set to be used throughout in order to illustrate the various analytic techniques. Chapter 3 introduces univariate statistics, the description of one variable at a time. Chapter 4 treats measures of association, the analysis of the relationship between two variables. Chapter 5 considers the statistical significance of the relationship between two variables. Chapter 6 focuses on simple regression, in which a dependent variable is influenced by an independent variable. Chapter 7 explicates multiple regression, in which a dependent variable is influenced by several independent variables. Chapter 8, by way of conclusion, offers analysis recommendations.

2. DATA GATHERING

Data, the raw stuff of analysis, come in a variety of forms. The researcher may conduct a public opinion survey, mail out a questionnaire, take notes from a statistical yearbook, make observations on the basis of library documents, or record impressions during fieldwork, to name a few. Regardless of the manner of collection, the data must be arranged numerically and stored, presumably in a computer, before analysis can commence. The *research question* guides the data process, which typically goes through the following stages:

I. Sample.
II. Measures.
III. Coding.
IV. Entry.
V. Checking.

Each of these stages is discussed below, in the context of a heuristic research example. Although data gathering is prelude to analysis, the importance of its proper execution cannot be overemphasized. (For an in-depth treatment of the data process, see Bourque & Clark, 1992.) The old saw, "garbage in, garbage out," rings true. No amount of sophisticated statistical manipulation will make up for the deficiencies of bad data.

The Research Question

Social scientists want to explain. What causes something to happen? Is it this, or is it that? How do I know? Well-trained researchers almost automatically think in terms of "cause and effect" when setting up a problem for investigation. They ponder possible explanations for the events observed, offering hypotheses or, more boldly, theories. To help sort out competing explanations, they apply statistical tests to data composed of empirical measures of relevant variables. A *variable* is simply something that varies in value. The variable to be explained, the "effect," is commonly called the *dependent variable,* generally labeled "Y." A possible "cause" is referred to as an *independent variable,* with the label "X." Suppose that, in the real world, X is indeed a positive cause of Y. In that case, we would expect data analysis to support the following *hypothesis,* "If X increases in value, then Y tends to increase in value." Of course, for reasons we will explore, the analysis might not yield this conclusion. The statistical test might be faulty or poorly interpreted, the victim of error or inadequate data. To appreciate the problems fully, let us develop a data example.

Our illustration draws on a topic of wide interest—academic ability. The overarching research question is "Why do some students do better than others?" In pursuit of an answer, we construct a hypothetical but realistic study. Suppose the Academic Affairs Office of Wintergreen College asks us to investigate the determinants of success on the 1st-year entrance exam and has provided funds for a student survey. Unfortunately, as is virtually always the case in social research, the available budget does not permit the entire *population* of interest (the incoming class) to be surveyed. Therefore, a *sample* must be drawn.

The Sample

A sample is representative of its population, within known limits, if it is a scientific, probability sample. The classic method here, which we employ, is *simple random sampling* (SRS). The population of the 1st-year class of Wintergreen College numbers 500. Our time and money allow us to interview about 1 in 10 of these students, yielding a sampling fraction of $\frac{1}{10}$. Therefore, from the alphabetical 1st-year student list provided by the Registrar, we select every tenth name, beginning with a random start number. (Technically, this method of sampling from a list is referred to as the *systematic selection procedure.* For coverage of sampling methodologies, see Kalton [1983].) Given that random start number is "7," then the seventh name down the list is chosen first, the seventeenth name chosen second, and so on, exhausting the list once 50 students are selected. This gives the *sample size,* written $N = 50$. As with any sampling situation, more observations could always be hoped for. Still, data-gathering costs cannot be ignored. Overall, this sample is large enough that we can speak with some confidence about the distributions and relationships of variables in the population, as shall be seen.

The Measures

The variables under investigation must be measured before any hypotheses can be tested. In this study, the dependent variable of Academic Ability is actually measured by student score on the 100-item entrance exam. In Table 2.1, column AA, we see the varying scores of the 50 students sampled. (A perfect score is 100, which none of these students obtained.) There are several independent variables, as several possible influences on student test performance are hypothesized. Many are measured in our special student survey, which consists of a 36-item questionnaire administered in face-to-face interviews lasting just under ½ hour. For example, a leading hypothesis holds that parents' education influences student performance. One of the student survey questions reads as follows:

"How many years of schooling would you say your mother received, all together?" [student answers in number of years].

A second item poses the same kind of question, asking about the father's education. The measure for the independent variable of Parents' Education is the average number of years of schooling for the mother and father (i.e., if the mother had 13 years and the father 11 years, then the Parents' Education score equals 12). Table 2.1, column PE lists the scores on the parents' education variable, among those surveyed.

The student survey yielded responses on other potential independent variables. One item, which served to form the variable Student Motivation, (Table 2.1, column SM), asks the student to evaluate his or her motivation to succeed in college, in the following way.

TABLE 2.1
Wintergreen College Data

Respondent Number	AA	PE	SM	AE	R	G	C
1	93	19	1	2	0	0	1
2	46	12	0	0	0	0	0
3	57	15	1	1	0	0	0
4	94	18	2	2	1	1	1
5	82	13	2	1	1	1	1
6	59	12	0	0	2	0	0
7	61	12	1	2	0	0	0
8	29	9	0	0	1	1	0
9	36	13	1	1	0	0	0
10	91	16	2	2	1	1	0
11	55	10	0	0	1	0	0
12	58	11	0	1	0	0	0
13	67	14	1	1	0	1	1
14	77	14	1	2	2	1	0
15	71	12	0	0	2	1	0
16	83	16	2	2	1	0	1
17	96	15	2	2	2	0	1
18	87	12	1	1	0	0	1
19	62	11	0	0	0	0	0
20	52	9	0	1	2	1	0
21	46	10	1	0	0	1	0
22	91	20	2	2	1	0	0
23	85	17	2	1	1	1	1
24	48	11	1	1	2	0	0
25	81	17	1	1	1	1	1
26	74	16	2	1	2	1	0
27	68	12	2	1	1	1	1
28	63	12	1	0	0	0	1
29	72	14	0	2	0	0	0
30	99	19	1	1	1	0	0
31	64	13	1	1	0	0	0
32	77	13	1	0	1	1	1
33	88	16	2	2	0	1	0
34	54	9	0	1	1	0	0
35	86	17	1	2	1	0	1
36	73	15	1	1	0	1	0
37	79	15	2	1	0	0	1
38	85	14	2	1	2	1	1
39	96	16	0	1	1	0	1
40	59	12	1	0	0	1	0
41	84	14	1	0	1	0	1

6

TABLE 2.1
Continued

Respondent Number	AA	PE	SM	AE	R	G	C
42	71	15	2	1	1	0	0
43	89	15	0	1	0	1	1
44	38	12	1	0	1	1	0
45	62	11	1	1	2	0	1
46	93	16	1	0	1	0	1
47	71	13	2	1	1	0	0
48	55	11	0	1	0	0	0
49	74	15	1	2	0	1	0
50	88	18	1	1	0	1	0

NOTE: AA = Academic Ability (number of items correct); PE = Parents' Education (average years); SM = Student Motivation (0 = not willing, 1 = undecided, 2 = willing); AE = Advisor Evaluation (0 = fail, 1 = succeed or fail, 2 = succeed); R = Religious Affiliation (0 = Catholic, 1 = Protestant, 2 = Jewish); G = Gender (0 = male, 1 = female); C = Community Type (0 = urban, 1 = rural).

"Some students put a lot of their free time into studies, even on the weekends. Others think their free time is their own. What about you? In terms of studying extra hours, would you say you are willing, not willing, or undecided?"

Besides Parents' Education and Student Motivation, other variables were measured in the survey, among them Gender (male or female), Religion (Catholic, Protestant, Jewish), and Community Type (urban or rural). These scores also are given in Table 2.1, columns G, R, and C respectively. Beyond these direct student survey data, we also have available information from the student's college admission application. Much of this admissions material seems of value for our study, such as the Academic Advisor's hand-written comments assessing the likelihood that the student will succeed in college. After evaluating the contents of these advisor remarks, we grouped them into a variable called Advisor Evaluation, with the following three prognosis categories, "likely to succeed," "could succeed or could fail," and "likely to fail."
This variable appears in Table 2.1 (column AE), along with the others we have discussed. Although they do not exhaust all the variables measured (or measurable) in our study, they do compose the bulk of the *data set* we analyze on subsequent pages.

Data Coding, Entry, and Checking

The values of the different variables should be efficiently stored, for ready computer use. For certain variables, the values to be recorded are obvious, consisting of the directly gathered numeric scores themselves. To take an example, it is evident that for the variable of Academic Ability (AA) the value to save is the point score (from 0 to 100) on the entrance test. Similarly with Parents' Education (PE), the number—average years of schooling—is the one to enter. However, for other variables, the value code (the symbol employed to indicate the value) is less obvious.

Look at the variable Student Motivation, for which the values are "willing," "not willing," and "undecided." In Table 2.1 (column SM) those numbered "2" indicate students who responded "willing," those numbered "1" actually responded "undecided," and the "0" responded "unwilling." These numbers are simply codes that when translated indicate the student's response category. Clearly, other numbers could have been used to designate a particular response without altering the intrinsic meaning of that response. For instance, if we substituted a "3" for the "2" code on this Student Motivation variable, that would not mark a more positive motivation; rather, it would just say that those who were recorded as "willing" now carry a different identification number. With the rest of the variables in our data set—Gender, Religion, Community Type, and Advisor Evaluation—we likewise observe that the specific values have numeric codes and understand that these numbers are merely placeholders.

In social science studies the observations on each case, with variable labels and codes, are routinely entered into a computer and stored in a data file. Indeed, Table 2.1 appears much like a typical data file from an interactive personal computer. Data files should always be carefully checked for *coding errors.* That is, were any of the variable values entered incorrectly? A review of the figures in Table 2.1 reveals, encouragingly, no *wild codes,* meaning no values outside of the possible range of scores on each variable (e.g., no one got a score of "103" on Academic Ability, or "8" on Student Motivation). However, a more subtle mistake, such as erroneous recording of a response category, could have taken place. For example, a student may have responded "willing" (code = 2) on Student Motivation but was improperly coded as "unwilling" (code = 0). To avoid such errors, each member of our research team checked the coding, achieving a high degree of intercoder reliability. We are confident that the data set contains few, if any, coding errors. Finally, although we have *missing data* (that is, no answer recorded) for a few of the individuals on a few of the items in the survey, there are no missing data for the variables of Table 2.1. (Perhaps surprisingly, there are no missing data on the religion variable, R. Each student in the sample selected one of these three alternatives.) Fortunately, our advance planning helped us develop the appropriate response categories and essentially eliminate the difficulties of refusal to answer. Had all this not been the case, and we were faced with an obvious missing data problem, the application of the analysis techniques developed in subsequent chapters would be of little use.

3. UNIVARIATE STATISTICS

The careful data analyst starts with an examination of the key features of each variable. Sometimes, the findings on the individual variables themselves yield critical insights. In any case, it gives an essential feel for the data. There are two aspects of any variable that merit special attention—*central tendency* and *dispersion*. The first concerns the variable's "typical" score, the second the spread of scores. Measures of central tendency unify the observations, providing them a summary meaning. Measures of dispersion tell how different the observations are, one from the other. Below, we treat the former, then the latter.

Central Tendency

The leading measures of central tendency are mean, median, and mode. The mean (technically the arithmetic mean) is the average value, the median the middle value, and the mode the most frequently occurring value. Take, as an example, the Academic Ability variable in our study (see Table 2.1, column AA). Its average score (the sum of the column AA numbers divided by 50) is 71.4. (We have rounded the score to the nearest tenth, from the computer-reported calculation of 71.38, in order to avoid giving a false sense of precision.) According to this measure, the "typical" student gets just over 70 out of the 100 possible points. How good a score is this? To get an idea, suppose those students scoring 90-100 were labeled "excellent," 80-89 " very good," and 70-79 "good," in terms of their prospects. One might conclude that the usual entering student at Wintergreen College does fairly well on the entrance exam, turning in at least a minimally "good" performance. Of course, this is valuable information for the incoming student and his or her parents.

The alternative measures confirm, in this instance, the initial impression of the typical student given by the mean. The median score, with half below and half above, is 72.5. (When the sample size is an even number, as it is here, the median actually represents an average of two "middle" cases, Nos. 25 and 26.) The mode of 71 yields a similar interpretation. If we were forced to select just one of these three measures to summarize the central tendency on this variable, we would probably pick the mean. For one reason, it is based on many more cases than the mode (which is actually the value for only three students, Nos. 15, 42, and 47). For another, the mean generally allows for more powerful inferential statistics, which will be pursued below.

The more precise the measurement, the more interpretable are these indicators of central tendency. *Quantitative* variables, such as age or income, have a high level of precision. The entrance-exam variable, for example, is measured at the quantitative level. That is, the scores are meaningful counts, whose units stand the same distance from each other. Thus someone with a score of 45 has correctly answered one less item than someone with 46 but one more than someone with 44. Here a score of 90 is double that of a score of 45. Quantitative variables have a valuable property—the mean, median, and mode are all informative.

For *qualitative* variables, these indicators of central tendency have less to say, because the measures themselves are less precise. There are two basic levels of qualitative variables: *ordinal* or *nominal*. The ordinal level of measurement ranks a case in terms of "more" or "less" of something, without saying exactly "how much more" or "how much less." Psychological attitudes are commonly measured at the ordinal level. For example, in our investigation, Student Motivation (see Table 2.1, column SM) is measured along an ordinal scale, from "willing " (code = 2), to "undecided" (code = 1), to "not willing" (code = 0). If one student says "willing," whereas another says "undecided," we conclude that the first student (ranked "2") is more motivated to study than the second (ranked "1"). However, we cannot go on to conclude that the first is twice as motivated as the second. (Put another way, we do not accept the results of the simple division of the rank scores, "2"/"1" = 2).

Because the scores on this ordinal variable are really ordered "codes" rather than interpretable counts, the average loses its sharp interpretation. For example, with the Student Motivation variable, the mean score equals 1.02. This number is but a rough guide to the typical amount of motivation possessed by the 1st-year student. It implies that, commonly, they fall in (or very near) the "undecided" category. However, the majority (i.e., 27 cases) were far from "undecided," placing themselves either in the "willing" or the "not willing" categories. The other measures of central tendency have somewhat more precision. The median equals "1." Remember that the median is the middle value. Looking at the *frequency distribution* of the variable, we observe 13 scored "0," 23 scored "1," and 14 scored "2." Hence, the middle individual falls within the second category. Finally, there is no ambiguity about the location of the mode, which is also "1."

The other level of qualitative variable, the nominal, is measured merely in terms of presence or absence of an attribute. Further, that attribute cannot be ordered, or scaled. Usual examples are region, gender, or religion. Our study records the Religious Affiliation of each student (see Table 2.1, column R). The variable has three categories—Catholic (code = "0"), Protestant (code = "1"), and Jewish (code = "2"). The scores have no meaning at all, other than to designate the student's religion. For instance, a "1" says the student is Protestant, not Catholic or Jewish; but that "1" does not mean that the student possesses more of something than a student with the score of "0." In other words, the scores do not imply any ordering of a property, from "more" to "less."

Because the scores on nominal variables are arbitrary, really just helping to name the variables, the calculation of the mean or the median makes no sense. However, the mode remains useful. In this case, the mode is "0." (There are 21 Catholics, compared to 20 Protestants and 9 Jews). Thus, to describe the central tendency of religion in this sample, we might remark that the modal student is Catholic; and it would probably be good to add that, as is often the case with the mode, that does not say it composes a majority.

Before leaving the topic of central tendency, the more favorable characteristics of a particular kind of nominal variable—the dichotomous—deserve mention. A dichotomous variable has two categories, here scored "1" and "0"; for example, Gender (1 = female, 0 = male) or Community Type (1 = rural, 0 = urban) in Table 2.1. With such variables, the average score has a meaningful interpretation. The average on the Gender variable equals .44, indicating the proportion of the sample that is female. Similarly, the average score for the Community Type variable is .40, which tells us that 40% of the students in the sample come from a rural background. Thus dichotomous variables can be treated mathematically as quantitative variables. As we shall see, this allows dichotomous variables a more flexible role in bivariate and multivariate analysis.

Dispersion

How spread out are the scores on a variable? In our particular study, how different are the students, looking at this and that variable? Are they very much alike? Or do they vary considerably in attitudes, behaviors, and characteristics? Two initial measures help answer these questions: range and concentration. For quantitative variables, range measures the distance from the highest to the lowest score. With the quantitative variable of Academic Ability, the range is 70 (i.e., 99 – 29). This wide range suggests, unsurprisingly, that the students differ greatly in their academic ability. For qualitative variables, the range is better understood as the count of the choices, or categories, recorded. To take an instance, the ordinal variable of Student Motivation records three responses ("not willing," "undecided," "willing"), as does the nominal variable of Religious Affiliation ("Catholic," "Protestant," "Jewish"). One observes that, in general, the score range on qualitative variables is restricted, compared to quantitative variables.

Concentration concerns the relative frequency of occurrence of a score. The more frequent a particular score relative to the others, the more concentrated the distribution on that value. With quantitative variables, there tends to be rather little concentration. For instance, with the Academic Ability variable, no score is repeated more than three times (and that occurs at 71). By way of contrast, concentration is generally higher with qualitative variables. Consider ordinal ones. At one extreme, when all the observations are at a single value, concentration is complete and spread is zero. At another extreme, when the values are divided evenly between the highest and lowest categories (say "0" or "2," leaving the middle "1" empty), then spread is maximized. The Student Motivation variable, as an illustration, resides between these extremes. It has 46% of its respondents at the middle category ("1"), with 26% on one side (at "0") and 28% on the other (at "2"). Although "undecided" is the most popular choice, more than half of the students still selected something else.

Finally, turn to the situation of the nominal variable. Zero spread occurs when all the values are in one category. However, concentration cannot be defined by an "empty middle," as it was in the ordinal case, because Religious Affilation is not ordered and therefore has no "middle." Instead, for a nominal variable, maximum spread occurs when all categories have the same number of observations. In our study, the Religious Affiliation variable appears a moderate distance from that theoretical maximum, with 41%, 40%, and 18% in the three categories. We might conclude that, along the dimension of religion, the sample has some diversity.

Range and concentration are but preliminary measures of dispersion. At least for quantitative variables, much more is possible. Below, we develop the standard deviation and related measures. (For ordinal and nominal variables, measures other than range and concentration exist, although they are less used and are beyond the space limitations of this monograph. Weisberg, 1992, provides a treatment of many measures of central tendency and spread, taking into account measurement level.) In research practice, the standard deviation is sometimes calculated and interpreted for ordinal (but never nominal) data. This controversial practice is likely to continue because it gives a sense, admittedly a crude one, of the general dispersion of an ordinal variable.

How spread out are values around a central, anchoring value? More particularly, given that the mean defines a variable's center, how dispersed are values around that center? Imagine the variable, years of adult education classes taken, measured on a small population of four long-time high school graduates, as follows: 2, 5, 7, 10. The mean of these scores equals 6 years. What is the spread of scores around this mean? A first impulse is simply to calculate the deviation of each value from the mean ($2 - 6 = -4$, $5 - 6 = -1$, $7 - 6 = 1$, $10 - 6 = 4$), then average. However, this strategy fails, always yielding an average deviation of zero, because the signed values (+ and −) cancel out ($[-4] + [-1] + [1] + [4] = 0$).

There are at least two ways to overcome this problem of the signs cancelling: take absolute values or square the values, before averaging. The first, the *average absolute deviation*, equals 2.5 in the current example. The second, the *average squared deviation*, otherwise known as the *variance*, equals 8.5 (i.e., $[-4]^2 + [-1]^2 + [4]^2 + [1]^2/4 = 8.5$). The advantage of the average absolute deviation is that it is readily understandable, indicating the typical distance from the mean, here 2.5 years. Its disadvantage is that it is almost useless mathematically, in terms of the statistical inference we eventually want to execute. In contrast, the average squared deviation, or variance, does have these desirable statistical properties. However, its disadvantage is that it has no intuitive meaning. For instance, in our example, the number 8.5 has no easy interpretation.

To overcome the disadvantages of both these measures, while maintaining something of their advantages, we calculate the *standard deviation*, which is simply the square root of the variance. In our example, the variance equals 8.5, yielding a square root of 2.9. The standard deviation, because it is derived from the variance, gives us the mathematical reach we seek. As well, it has intuitive meaning. Note that in our example, the standard deviation value is just slightly larger than the average absolute deviation (2.9 > 2.5). In general, the average absolute deviation of a variable is around four-fifths the size of the standard deviation (Mohr, 1990, p. 11). Thus we can interpret the standard deviation as equivalent, in a rough way, to the average distance of an observation from the mean.

Almost always, we calculate the standard deviation on a variable from a sample, rather than a population. In that case, it is desirable to adjust the general formula just a bit, by subtracting one case from the denominator, as follows:

$$S_X = \sqrt{\frac{\sum (X_i - \overline{X})^2}{N - 1}}$$ [3.1]

where S_X is the standard deviation estimated from the sample, $\sum$ indicates the need to sum, X_i are the observations on the variable X, $\overline{X}$ is the the mean of the observations on X, and N is the sample size.

This correction, dividing by $N - 1$ rather than N, is necessary for the estimator to be unbiased. (Technically, we have used up 1 *degree of freedom* in computing the sample mean. That is, the N observed values must now add up to N multiplied by that estimated mean. This constrains one observation but leaves $N - 1$ "free.") Although this is an important correction in terms of statistical theory, it has a negligible impact on the interpretation, especially as sample size increases.

In our study of students at Wintergreen College, recall the sample size, $N = 50$. We might wish we could afford a somewhat larger sample. However, we see that even a sample of this size, because it is a scientific probability sample, allows informative estimates. The values on the Academic Ability variable have a standard deviation of 17.4, suggesting the typical student falls a fair distance from the mean score of 71.4. In other words, on the basis of this standard deviation we judge there is a good amount of spread in their performance, reinforcing the initial impression given by the range of scores.

The standard deviation allows an even more precise estimate of the spread of scores if the distribution of the population variable can be assumed to follow a normal curve, such as that sketched in Figure 3.1. In that case, it works out mathematically that about 68% of the cases can be expected to have scores + or − 1 standard deviation from the mean, 95% within + or − 2 standard deviations. (Beyond these 2 standard deviations, or more technically 1.96 standard deviations, then, you can expect to find the remaining 5% of the cases.) Applying these rules to the Academic

14

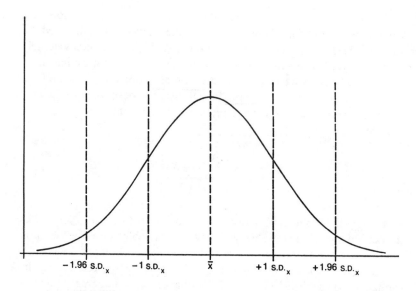

Note: S.D.$_x$ = standard deviation of population variable, x
$\bar{x}$ = mean of population variable, x

Figure 3.1. A Normal Curve

Ability variable, this gives the expectation that about 68% of the entering students scored between 88.8 and 54.0 (i.e., 71.4 + or − 17.4). Again, our assessment that the students vary considerably in their ability is confirmed.

Of course, the quality of this assessment about the variability of scores is not independent of the validity of the normality assumption. Is the variable under study normally distributed? In particular, what about entrance exam scores in our student population? The sample at hand provides evidence on this question. There are various tools for assessing normality. A visual representation of the data, especially a *histogram*, is helpful. In Figure 3.2, one observes a bar graph, a histogram of the distribution of values on the Academic Ability variable. On the horizontal axis range the exam scores, grouped into four categories of values, from low to high. On the vertical axis is indicated the proportion of cases in the sample that belong within the specific bar. In general, if a distribution is perfectly normal, a bell-shaped curve superimposed over its histogram fits rather

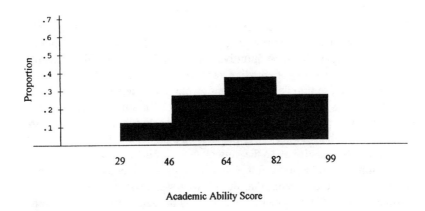

Figure 3.2. Histogram for the Academic Ability Variable

nicely, the bars tending to fill in symmetrically the area underneath the curve and the curve itself cutting the top of each bar at the midpoint.

The histogram of Figure 3.2, for the data on entrance exam scores, does not conform flawlessly to the contours of a normal curve. However, it is hump-shaped, with dispersed values and a single mode (i.e., one clearly highest bar). Further, although it has a slight negative skew (a bit over-loaded with values on the right-hand tail), it is not terribly skewed. Because it is from a sample, we might expect it to be less than perfectly normal, even if the variable were normal in the population. Also, the vagaries of histogram construction, which require the analyst to select the number of bars and their cutoff points, inevitably introduce error. (Readers should experiment with the different histogram commands in a standard statistical package and see for themselves how much the shape can change even working with the same data.)

Graphic representations of actual data, valuable as they are, virtually never reveal precisely the underlying theoretical distribution. They give us an important clue to it but need to be evaluated in the context of certain statistical tests. So, more quantitatively, how far off normal is the underlying distribution likely to be? A lot or a little? A simple but powerful test compares the central tendency measures. If a variable is normal, then the mean, the median, and the mode are equal. Here we see that the mean is 71.4, the median is 72.5, and the mode is 71. These values, which are almost identical, suggest that the mathematical distribution is close to normal, after all.

A further calculation, the *skewness statistic,* reinforces this conclusion. Its formula essentially says to cube the *standard scores* (see next chapter), sum them, then calculate the average (Lewis-Beck, 1980, p. 29). Although this formula permits little intuitive understanding, it has the valuable mathematical property of equaling zero when the distribution is perfectly normal. For these sample observations on entrance exam scores, skewness = −.42. How is this number to be evaluated? It is certainly not zero, which would suggest perfect normality. In general, as a distribution departs more from normal, the skewness statistic takes on a higher and higher value, but the skewness statistic has no theoretical upper limit (such as 1.0). This lack of an upper boundary does not pose a great problem, because it has been found, as a rule-of-thumb, that the skewness statistic must exceed .8 in absolute value before the distribution actually becomes "noticeably skewed" (Bourque & Clark, 1992, p. 69). The absolute value in this particular case (of .42) is rather far from that ceiling, suggesting skewness is no more than mild. (This conclusion is reinforced by an experimental effort to improve normality in the sample by the customary method of logging the variable. This actually made the distribution less normal, yielding a skewness of −1.02. The natural log and other transformations are discussed below.)

Taken together, the skewness statistics, the histogram, and the mean-median-mode comparison indicate that the normality assumption is not wide of the mark and allows useful information to be gleaned about the probable dispersion of Academic Ability in the population under study. Of course, the normality assumption cannot automatically be invoked, nor is it always needed. Its utilization requires good defense, in the specific context of the research questions being asked.

Central Tendency, Dispersion, and Outliers

Outliers are values that do not seem to go with the others. Suppose this series of values for years of age on variable *Q*: 6, 9, 12, 14, 18, 23, 88. The last value, 88, lies well out from the next highest (23), appearing separated from the cluster of other observations on age. Outliers can have a serious influence on our measures. In this simple example, the mean equals 24.3, clearly a poor summary measure of the typical age score on variable *Q*. With such an outlier problem, a better indicator of central tendency is the median value, at 14. Outliers can also affect dispersion measures. Here, most obviously, the range, 88 − 6 = 82, is misleading. Once the outlier is excluded the spread is really rather narrow, 23 − 6 = 17. More generally, outliers may make a distribution terribly skewed, moving it very far from the useful ideal of a normal curve.

Outliers can render data generalizations tricky. What, if anything, should be done? First, it needs to be established that an outlier really is an outlier. Sometimes a coding error is responsible for the appearance of an outlier. In our above example, with variable Q, it may have been that we mistakenly coded an "88," instead of an actual "8." Such mistakes are not hard to make and ought to be ruled out before going on. Assuming the suspect value is not the product of a coding error, then ask, Is the value truly inconsistent with the other values? Some judgment is involved here. Nevertheless, statistical guidelines are helpful. Remember that if a variable follows a normal curve, then the expectation is that 5% of the values will lie beyond 2 standard deviations from the mean. Thus we should not automatically be surprised when some of the values are extreme. Instead, we might ask how many are there, how far out are they, and what is the underlying distribution? It may be that, after all, at least probabilistically, they are consistent with the other values.

Suppose these various considerations lead to the conclusion that the values in question are indeed outliers. Then, four basic approaches are possible: (a) remove, (b) transform, (c) leave as they are, or (d) report results with and without outliers. Let us evaluate each, in turn. The first strategy, of removal, simply eliminates an outlier from further analysis. This is not recommended in isolation, because it just hides the problem. Outliers represent information, perhaps important, about the population sampled. If they are totally excluded, it is not even clear what population is being discussed. Never throw away good data.

The strategy of transformation finds favor over removal, in that these unusual data are not ignored altogether. With above variable Q, we might apply a square root transformation to the values, yielding 2.4, 3, 3.5, 3.7, 4.2, 9.4. The case with the score of 88 is not removed, but instead its value is transformed to its square root of 9.4. Observe that 9.4 is much less of an outlier (in the transformed series) than was 88 (in the untransformed series). This transformation "pulled in" the outlying value and made it more consistent with the other values.

Another widely used transformation that also tends to "pull in" outlying values is the logarithmic transformation. (Recall that the logarithm of a number is the power of a base necessary to yield the original number. For example, the log of the number 100 is 2, when the base is 10. In addition to base 10 yielding a *common log,* there is base e yielding a *natural log.* Common logs may be readily converted to natural logs, and vice versa.) A difficulty with these transformations, and variable transformations in general, is that the new values do not always have a meaningful interpretation. For example, original variable Q, measured in years of age, has a ready meaning. However, transformed variable Q is measured in the square root of years of age, which has no intuitive sense. For reasons of interpretation, then, analysts sometimes avoid transformations. Still, they should recognize that the original value can be retrieved, if so desired. For instance here, when the square root score is squared, we are back to the original age in years. (Also, variable transformations are sometimes useful for other purposes, as shall be seen in the multiple regression chapter.)

The third strategy simply recognizes the outliers but makes no attempt to exclude or alter them. The argument is straightforward. Because the study is well designed, with a large random sample and good measures, the outliers are to be trusted as representing genuine values in the population. That they may affect the statistics on central tendency and dispersion is in the nature of things and should be duly reported, even if the task of generalization is made more difficult.

To pursue strictly the third strategy, the analyst must be brimming with confidence. Sometimes, analysts worry over outliers in spite of themselves. In such a situation, the fourth strategy especially recommends itself. It says to calculate the statistics of interest with and without the outliers (transformed or not), then compare the results. It may be that the outliers, even though present, do not influence in an important way the conclusions the analyst wishes to draw. For example, the mean may be of almost the same magnitude as the median, even though outliers are observed. This could easily occur, of course, in the presence of a sufficiently large sample. Or, to take another example, the standard deviation may indicate that the values on the variable are greatly spread out, a substantively interesting conclusion that holds regardless of whether the analyst takes into account the outliers. The suggestion, then, is that it is occasionally worthwhile to report results both with and without outliers included. In this way, the reader is provided full information. The conclusion may be that, happily, there is finally not an outlier problem, in that the relevant interpretations hold across both. Or, if the interpretations differ, then they are there to suggest further data gathering and diagnosis.

4. MEASURES OF ASSOCIATION

The central question, for much social science research, is how one variable relates to another. Does social class have anything to do with political participation? If there is a relationship between class and politics, is it strong? Although these are questions from a specific area of research in political sociology, they represent a broader, generic, set. How does variable X relate to variable Y? Is that relationship strong? Below we offer different measures of bivariate association in order to help answer these questions.

Correlation

When two variables are related, changes in one tend to accompany changes in the other. Suppose that as the values on X become higher, we observe that the values on Y generally become higher. We would conclude that there was a positive relationship between X and Y. This seems to be the nature of the relationship between Parents' Education and Academic Ability, according to the *scatterplot* of our sample data from the Wintergreen College study in Figure 4.1.

Academic Ability scores are arrayed on the Y axis, Parents' Education scores on the X axis. The dots represent the students in the survey. Imagine each is located by the intersection of perpendicular lines, respectively, from

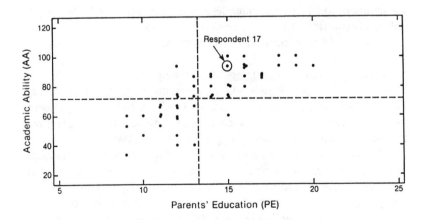

Figure 4.1. Scatterplot of Academic Ability and Parents' Education

its value on each axis. For example, Student Respondent No. 17 has a Parents' Education score of 15 and an Academic Ability score of 96, thus fixing a unique spot on the graph. This scatter of points suggests a positive relationship, because it appears that students who have high values on Parents' Education usually have high values on Academic Ability.

We can make a more precise visual assessment by dividing the scatterplot into four quadrants, based on location above or below the respective mean scores ($\overline{Y}$ = 71.4, $\overline{X}$ = 13.8). If the relationship is positive, the expectation is that those students who are above average on X will mostly be above average on Y. We see from the northeast quadrant that this expectation is borne out. Also, the other quadrants lend support to this overall assessment of the relationship.

The visual impression that X and Y vary together, or *covary*, is confirmed (or not) in a single summary statistic, known as the *covariance*. The following formula calculates the sample covariance, s_{XY}, between variables X and Y:

$$s_{XY} = \text{Covariance}_{XY} = \frac{\sum (X_i - \overline{X})(Y_i - \overline{Y})}{N - 1} . \qquad [4.1]$$

The covariance statistic systematically uses all the deviations from the means (like those observed in the quadrants). The products of these deviations are summed, then averaged. (Actually, the division by $N - 1$ makes it a bit greater than an average for the particular sample. Again, we are reminded to take into account degrees of freedom, in order to have an unbiased estimator.) The covariance estimate between Parents' Education and Academic Ability equals 37.82, confirming their positive relationship in this sample.

The covariance is valuable for determining the sign (+, −, 0) of a relationship. However, it says nothing about the strength of relationship. For example, does the above estimate of 37.82 indicate a strong association? How can we answer? The covariance statistic just produces a raw number, which has no theoretical upper bound. It can take on a larger value simply from a change in the measurement unit of a variable. For instance, if Parents' Education is scored in semesters (i.e., 1 year equals two semesters), then the estimated covariance becomes 75.64. Obviously, the relationship between Parents' Education and Academic Ability has not changed, suddenly doubling in strength. The larger number is merely an artifact of the scoring change from years to semesters. What is needed is a summary statistic of relationship impervious to measurement unit, with a theoretical and intuitive boundary. The *correlation coefficient* is that statistic.

It is helpful to think of the correlation coefficient as the covariance calculated with variables converted into standard deviation units. To convert the scores of a variable to these *standard scores,* as they are called, the deviations from the mean (see a numerator variable in Equation 4.1 above) are divided by the standard deviation. As an example, take the very simple data set from the last chapter, in which the population variable, years of adult education classes, had original scores of 2, 5, 7, and 10. The mean of these scores was 6, yielding deviations from the mean, respectively, of −4, −1, 1, and 4. Recalling the standard deviation was 2.9, we can now convert these raw deviations to standard scores: (−4/2.9) = −1.38; (−1/2.9) = −.34; (1/2.9) = .34; and (4/2.9) = 1.38. The variation in the variable is now measured from the central value of the mean and is expressed in standard deviation units. We see, for instance, that the person with an original score of 10 years is over 1 standard deviation unit (precisely, 1.38) above the mean (of 6 years). Once the scores on the variables are calibrated in terms of standard deviation units (as they are in the numerator in the formula below), the magnitude of the covariance becomes immune to change in the original units of measurement.

In the following formula, the *sample correlation coefficient,* symbolized by the letter "*r*," merely equals the sample covariance computed on standard score, or standardized, variables.

$$r_{XY} = \frac{\sum \left(\frac{X_i - \overline{X}}{S_X}\right)\left(\frac{Y_i - \overline{Y}}{S_Y}\right)}{N-1} \qquad [4.2]$$

where r_{XY} is the sample correlation coefficient; S_X, S_Y are the sample standard deviations; X, Y are sample variables; and N is sample size.

The correlation coefficient has a theoretical boundary of +1 (or −1), indicating a perfect linear relationship. If $r = 0$, then X and Y appear linearly unrelated. In our college study, the sample correlation between Parents' Education and Academic Ability equals .79, a rather strong relationship.

It is important to note that the correlation coefficient measures the degree of *linearity* in a relationship. If we look again at Figure 4.1, we can easily imagine a line running through the scatterplot, with most of the points rather close to it. Here the correlation coefficient captures well the relationship between X and Y. This need not be the case. (Alternative, nonlinear relationships are discussed in Chapter 7.) If the relationship is not linear, the correlation cofficient poorly estimates it and should not be applied. Obviously, to aid in assessment of the linearity, the scatterplot should always be consulted.

The term "correlation" is a common shorthand, and used without quali- fication it virtually always refers to the above coefficient. "Pearson's r," as it is often called (after the biologist who led its development at the end of the 19th century), has received more application than any other measure of association. It remains the ideal bivariate measure for quantitative variables. Further, it gets heavy use with ordinal variables; but, in a strict sense, application of Pearson's r to data measured at the ordinal level violates assumptions necessary for sound inference. Therefore, when the data are less than quantitative, alternative measures of association merit consideration. Below we examine relationships among ordinal data, even- tually offering *tau* as a useful measure. Then we explore nominal data, offering *lambda* as a useful measure there.

Ordinal Data: The Tau Measure of Association

Assuming two variables are measured at the ordinal level, how should we begin to assess their relationship? The impulse of the novice may be to start with the scatterplot. Unfortunately, scatterplots of ordinal data gener- ally reveal next to nothing about the presence of a relationship, let alone its strength. (Doubtful readers are invited to demonstrate this conclusion for themselves.) The difficulty resides with the level of measurement— there are so few alternative values on X and Y that a pepper of dots well-spread over the grid is impossible. Instead, what is typically observed are dense bunches of points on a scarce number of sites, all dumb to interpretation.

With ordinal data analysis, the *contingency table* takes over from the scatterplot as a preliminary means of evaluating the relationship. In Table 4.1a, we observe a *cross-tabulation* of Student Motivation and Advisor Evaluation. It is a 3×3 table, with at least five cases in each of the cells, except for two. (There is only one student with a [0, 2] combination—"not willing" on motivation but judged likely to "succeed" by the advisor—and no student with a [2, 0] combination—"willing"on motivation but judged likely to "fail" by the advisor.) At the top of the table is the column variable, customarily regarded as independent (X). At the side is the row variable, customarily regarded as dependent (Y). The theoretical argument is that

TABLE 4.1a

The Observed Relationship Between Student Motivation
and Advisor Evaluation, Total $N = 50$

Advisor Evaluation	Student Motivation		
	Not Willing	Undecided	Willing
Fail	46%	30%	0%
	(6)	(7)	(0)
Undecided	46%	48%	57%
	(6)	(11)	(8)
Succeed	8%	22%	43%
	(1)	(5)	(6)
Total	100%	100%	100%

NOTE: The figures in parentheses are the raw frequencies within each cell. The percentage above the raw frequency shows what percentage of those in that particular independent variable category also found themselves in that particular dependent variable category. For example, among those in the Student Motivation category of "willing," 43% were judged as likely to "succeed" by their Academic Advisor. Each column of percentages sums to 100%.

more self-motivated students (X) should be evaluated more positively by advisors (Y); thus the hypothesis: as X increases, Y tends to increase.

A first test of this hypothesis comes from evaluation of *percentage differences*. The test is straightforward, provided the table is clearly set up, with the independent variable at the top. (A common mistake is to place it in the row, then attempt to apply the test as if it were in the column. Always check to see that the independent variable is the column variable.) In each column is a percentage frequency distribution, summing to 100%. It indicates the percentage who selected the different dependent variable categories, given the particular independent variable category. For example, within the independent variable category of "not willing" on Student Motivation (score of 0, column 1), 46% have an Advisor Evaluation of likely to "fail" (score of 0); another 46% have an "undecided" Advisor Evaluation, that is, could either "succeed or fail" (score of 1); and the remaining 8% have an Advisor Evaluation of likely to "succeed" (score of 2).

If Student Motivation makes a difference, as hypothesized, we would expect the percentage of high advisor evaluations to be greater among the more highly motivated students. Is this so? To answer the question, read left-to-right across the third row, the highest Advisor Evaluation category. As Student Motivation increases (0 to 1, "not willing" to "undecided"), the

TABLE 4.1b
A Hypothetical Perfect Ordinal Relationship Between
Student Motivation and Advisor Evaluation, Total $N = 50$

Advisor Evaluation	Student Motivation		
	Not Willing	Undecided	Willing
Fail	100% (13)		
Undecided		100% (23)	
Succeed			100% (14)
Total	100%	100%	100%

NOTE: The terms in the table are defined as in Table 4.1a.

percentage in this highest advisor category goes from 8 to 22 (for a percentage difference of +14). As X increases again (1 to 2, "undecided" to "willing"), so does the highest advisory percentage, from 22 to 43 (for a percentage difference of +21). The more motivated these students see themselves, the better ratings their advisors are likely to give them. To take the extremes, among students with low motivation, only 8% are likely to receive a high advisor evaluation, in contrast to 43% among the highly motivated students. This yields a not inconsequential percentage difference of 35 points (i.e., $43 - 8$).

Overall, these percentage differences suggest that the relationship between X and Y is not trivial. Further, it is not perfect, as would be suggested if "100%" were the frequency recorded in each diagonal cell, as illustrated in the hypothetical relationship in Table 4.1b. (Here, a move to a higher category on X is always accompanied by a move to a higher category on Y). Between the boundaries—"not trivial" and "not perfect"—what is the proper description? Unfortunately, the percentage differences do not offer a summary answer. For one, the percentage difference between one particular cell and another ignores the other cell values and the differences between them. The problem of generalizing about the relationship increases as the table becomes larger. With almost any table larger than 2×2, a resort to summary measures of association is necessary. Perhaps the most useful is Kendall's tau, developed below. (See the discussions in Liebetrau, 1983, pp. 49-51, 70, and Gibbons, 1993, pp. 11-15.)

Think about the respondents to a survey, a pair at a time. Suppose respondents i and j, each with scores on variables X and Y. As one possibility, $X_i > X_j$ and $Y_i > Y_j$ yields a *concordant pair* of cases. For example, one student scores higher on Student Motivation than another particular student, and also scores higher on Advisor Evaluation. Such a pair of students "concords with" our hypothesis, so to speak. As another possibility, $X_i > X_j$ but $Y_i < Y_j$ yields a *discordant pair* of cases. Imagine one student who scores better than another on Student Motivation but does more poorly on Advisor Evaluation, and thus is "in disaccord with" our hypothesis. Yet another possibility is $X_i = X_j$ (or $Y_i = Y_j$). Such a pair is considered a *tie*. For example, two particular students have the same motivation score, so are neither in accord or disaccord. In general, concordant, discordant, and tied pairs can be defined as those for which $(X_j - X_i)$ multiplied by $(Y_j - Y_i)$ is positive, negative, or zero, respectively.

After grasping the notion of concordance, Kendall's tau measure becomes intuitively straightforward. "Tau-a" takes all concordant pairs, C, and subtracts from them all discordant pairs, D, dividing that by the number of all possible pairs ($N[N - 1]/2$). Although tau-a is engagingly simple, it fails to take into account tied pairs, which are almost always present. Further, in their presence it can no longer attain the desirable theoretical bound of $+1.0$ (or -1.0). Therefore, we turn to tau-b, which corrects for such ties, as seen in the following formula (Liebetrau, 1983, p. 69),

$$\text{tau--b} = \frac{(C - D)}{\sqrt{(C + D + T_X)(C + D + T_Y)}} \qquad [4.3]$$

where C are concordant pairs, D are discordant pairs, T_X are pairs tied on X, and T_Y are pairs tied on Y.

When a table is square, that is, has an equal number of rows and columns, then tau-b has the desirable theoretical boundary of $+1.0$, or -1.0. (To maintain this theoretical boundary when the table is not square, the analyst may prefer to report a somewhat adjusted coefficient, *tau-c*, which usually yields a number of slightly different magnitude.) For a perfect relationship, such as that depicted in the 3×3 of Table 4.1b, the tau-b = 1.0. At the hypothetical opposite, if X and Y were independent of each other, then tau-b = 0. Applied to the actual data example of Table 4.1a, we observe that tau-b = .38. This indicates, overall, a moderate positive relationship between Student Motivation and Advisor Evaluation.

TABLE 4.1c
A Hypothetical Nonmonotonic Relationship Between
Student Motivation and Advisor Evaluation, Total $N = 50$

Advisor Evaluation	Student Motivation Not Willing	Student Motivation Undecided	Student Motivation Willing
Fail	100% (13)		
Undecided			100% (14)
Succeed		100% (23)	
Total	100%	100%	100%

NOTE: The terms in the table are defined as in Table 4.1a.

Recall that with Pearson's r, appropriate application depended on the assumption that the relationship estimated was linear. With ordinal variables, relationships generally lack linear precision. However, they are required to be *monotonic*. For example, when a relationship is positive-monotonic, increases in X tend to be accompanied by increases in Y. (It is not expected, though, that each increase in X produces the same numerical increase in Y. Thus the monotonic condition is broader, or looser, than the linearity condition.) Obviously, a relationship between two ordinal variables need not be monotonic, as the example of Table 4.1c shows.

Here one observes, in this hypothetical example, that higher X values do not always tend to lead to higher Y values. Instead, an increase from the second X rank to the third actually accompanies a drop in the rank of Y. The relationship between X and Y, even though perfectly predictable, is *nonmonotonic*. In this case, an ordinal measure of association, such as a tau-b, would poorly represent this relationship. An alternative might be to simply treat the variables as nominal and apply a nominal measure of association, such as we discuss below.

Nominal Data: Goodman and Kruskals' Lambda

In assessing the relationship between two nominal variables, it generally makes no sense to apply an ordinal measure of association such as tau-b.

TABLE 4.2

The Observed Relationship Between Community Type and Religious
Affiliation, Total $N = 50$

	Community Type	
Religious Affiliation	Urban	Rural
Catholic	50%	30%
	(15)	(6)
Protestant	30%	55%
	(9)	(11)
Jewish	20%	15%
	(6)	(3)
Total	100%	100%

NOTE: The terms in the table are defined as in Table 4.1a.

Because nominal variables lack the ordering property of "more or less" of
something, the phrase "as X increases, Y tends to increase" has no meaning.
Still, nominal variables may be related, and that relationship may be strong
or weak. How is that relationship to be evaluated? We can begin, as with
the ordinal case, by examining the frequencies in a contingency table. In
Table 4.2 is the cross-tabulation of two nominal variables from our college
study—student's Community Type (urban = 0, rural = 1) and student's
Religious Affiliation (Catholic = 0, Protestant = 1, Jewish = 2).

One hypothesis is that, because of settlement patterns, Religious Affiliation can be predicted, at least to some extent, from Community Type.
Therefore, in the table, Community Type is placed at the top in the
independent variable (X) position, and Religious Affiliation (Y) is at the
side. Are the two variables associated? Look at percentage differences
(reading across). Fully 55% of the rural students are Protestant, as compared to 30% of urban students, for a percentage difference of 25 points.
This suggests some link. However, the other comparable percentage differences are less pronounced, at only 20 points for Catholics and 5 points
for Jews. Overall, these percentage differences do not give a clear description of the relationship between community and religion. What is needed
is a summary measure of association, such as Goodman and Kruskals'
lambda (λ) developed below (Liebetrau, 1983, pp. 16-24).

Lamba (λ) is a predictive measure of association whose calculation and
interpretation are pleasingly straighforward. It tells us how much we can

reduce our error in predicting Y, once we know X. Consider further the data of Table 4.2. First suppose you wish to predict each student's religion knowing only the overall frequency distribution of Y (of 21 Catholics, 20 Protestants, and 9 Jews). Then, to minimize error, you must always predict the religion in the category with the largest frequency; that is, Catholic, with 21 students. Such an information-poor prediction strategy generates considerable error, namely the 29 students who are not Catholic.

Now imagine that you are also provided the information on the X values, which allows knowledge of the frequency distribution of Y *within each X category.* To mimimize prediction error, you follow the same strategy as before, always picking the religion category that has the largest frequency. Within the Urban category of X, that choice is still Catholic (at 15); but within the Rural category it becomes Protestant (at 11). What is the new prediction error? For the Urban category, it is 15 (i.e., the 9 Protestants plus the 6 Jews). For the Rural category, it is 9 (i.e., the 6 Catholics plus the 3 Jews). This yields a combined error of 24 (i.e., 15 + 9). Overall, knowing X reduced total prediction error by 5 (i.e., 29 − 24). The proportional reduction in prediction error is labeled lambda. Here, lambda = 5/29 = .17. In general, we may write

$$\lambda = \frac{\text{reduction in prediction errors knowing } X}{\text{prediction errors not knowing } X}. \qquad [4.4]$$

Possible values of lambda range from 1.0 to 0. At the one extreme, if lambda = 1.0, then knowing X allows flawless prediction of Y. At the other extreme, if lambda = 0, then knowing X is no help at all. In our example, where lambda = .17, we observe that knowledge of the student's Community Type seems to help little predictively, only enabling five more student religions to be guessed correctly. It is safe to conclude that the relationship between Community Type and Religious Affiliation is mild, at best.

Dichotomous Variables: Flexibility of Choice

Recall that a dichotomous variable may be treated mathematically at any measurement level—quantitative or qualitative. Generally speaking, we wish to use the highest level. Greater precision is afforded as we move up the ladder from nominal to ordinal to quantitative. Thus when X and Y are both dichotomous, we legitimately employ a Pearson's r. Further, if one of the two variables is a dichotomy, say X, then the association choice is constrained only by the measurement level of Y: (a) if Y were a nominal variable with multiple categories, then lambda would still be preferred; (b) if Y were ordinal, then a tau would be appropriate; and (c) if Y were quantitative, then an r could be calculated. The data of our study provide one example of the last case. The variable of Gender is a dichotomy (female = 1, male = 0). Does gender relate to the quantitative variable of Academic Ability? We may, appropriately, correlate these two variables, and obtain $r = .04$.

As it turns out, the correlation between gender and ability is tiny, quite close to zero. Indeed, in the population of students, it may not even exist. Clearly, it would seem difficult to argue against the notion that there is no real link between the two variables, on the basis of these sample results. It is easy to believe that, just by chance, the number ".04" popped up. In fact, a test would show that the result was not "significant." But what does that mean? To comprehend such a statement, we need to understand significance testing, which is taken up in the next chapter.

Summary and Conclusion

Often, the social science researcher wishes to measure the association between two variables. Computer statistical packages have greatly aided this effort, almost too much so. For instance, when you simply "ask the computer" to print out a contingency table and list "all statistics," what results is an inundation of coefficients. We propose that rather than getting "all statistics," you request certain ones based on your hypotheses and the level of measurement of the variables. In general, quantitative measurement calls for Pearson's r, ordinal measurement calls for tau, and nominal measurement calls for lambda.

Of course, these choices do not exhaust the realm of bivariate measures of association, and their exclusive application risks neglect of subtleties in the data, such as the presence of nonmonotonicity, something an exploration of percentage differences might reveal. Nevertheless, on the basis of statistical theory as well as research practice, we conclude that these measures are generally as good as, or better than, others. With regard to quantitative measures, Pearson's r is really without rival. However, at the ordinal level, tau has some competitors (see the evaluation in Gibbons, 1993). In practice, a leading competitor is Goodman and Kruskals' gamma. The difficulty with gamma is that it "inflates" the relationship, making it appear bigger than it is. In particular, it will virtually always register a larger magnitude than tau. As a case in point, from our report of the relationship between Student Motivation and Advisor Evaluation, tau-b = .38 but gamma = .58. This rather gross inflation is not atypical and comes from its neglect of "tied" pairs in the calculation. (This neglect is evident from the formula, gamma = [concordant pairs − discordant pairs]/[concordant pairs + discordant pairs]. See the discussion in Gibbons, 1993, pp. 69-70.)

With respect to nominal measures, Cramer's V, derived from the chi-square statistic (discussed in the next chapter), is sometimes offered as an alternative to lambda (Liebetrau, 1983, pp. 14-16). Like lambda, it has a theoretical range in value from 0 to 1. In our study, the relationship between Community Type and Religious Affiliation yields a Cramer's V of .25, a bit larger in absolute value than lambda. The difficulty with Cramer's V is that it lacks the clear interpretation lambda affords. It says something generally about whether an association exists between X and Y but tells us little about predictive power or error reduction.

5. SIGNIFICANCE TESTING

In our research, we almost always use a sample in order to inform ourselves about a population. Assuming a probability sample (classically, a simple random sample), we gain confidence in our statistical inferences concerning the *population parameters*—the true values under study. But how much confidence is gained? To be specific, how much do the measures of association calculated on our student study sample—Pearson's r, tau-b, lambda—tell us about the real relationships among these variables? For instance, does the tau-b = .38 register the association between the Student Motivation and the Academic Evaluation variables in the entire 1st-year class? Because it is a sample, we would expect intuitively that this estimate is not exactly right. But how far off can we say it is? Could the true value be larger, say .59? Or smaller, say .17? Could it even be near .00, with the two variables actually barely linked?

Whenever we examine the relationship between variables X and Y in a sample, we face the overriding question, "Is it statistically significant?" If the answer is "yes," then we are reassured about a hypothesis relating the two. If the answer is "no," then we may doubt that they have anything to do with each other. Although an understanding of significance testing is immensely important, its explanation can quickly become hard to follow. Below, the logic of significance testing is initially developed through estimation of that simplest of population parameters—the mean. Such a background makes it easy to grasp the interpretation of significance tests for the more complex, bivariate measures of association. (For a full treatment of significance testing, see Mohr, 1990.)

The Logic: A Simple Example

By way of illustration, let us explore another variable that happens also to be measured in our Wintergreen College study—Library Book Returns. For each of the 50 students, we have available the library record of the dates they took out and returned books. The regulation checkout time is 6 weeks. Our theoretical interest is in the degree of delinquency with regard to library use, as indicated by late returns. (There is also a policy concern, with some administrators feeling that the 6-week checkout encourages abuse.) Every student surveyed was assigned a current Library Book Return score, equal to the number of days early (–) or late (+) they brought back their last book. (Thus a student who was 3 days overdue would receive a score of +3, whereas a student who turned in the book 2 days early would receive a score of –2.)

One hypothesis is that the typical 1st-year student is rule-abiding and returns books right on time, in which case the average Library Book Return score would equal zero. An alternative is that 1st-year students generally fail to return books on time, in which case the average Library Book Return score will be greater than zero. (An opposite alternative, even if remote, is that they actually tend to return the books early, yielding a score less than zero.) These compose two hypotheses—a null and an open-ended alternative—about μ_X (mu X), the mean of Library Book Return days (variable X) in the 1st-year student population: that mean is zero or it is not. We may write

$$H_0: \mu_X = 0$$

$$H_1: \mu_X \neq 0$$

In our sample, suppose we estimate the mean of Library Book Return days as $\overline{X} = 7$. That estimate is not zero, but it is not large enough that, intuitively, we would rule out a zero population value. (We have sampled only 50 students, and 1 week late on a 6-week book is not far off the mark, at least some might argue.) Formally to reject the null (or to fail to do so),

32

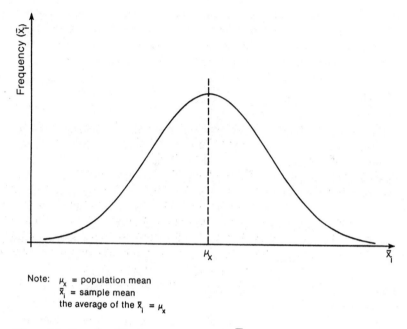

Note: μ_x = population mean
$\bar{x}_i$ = sample mean
the average of the $\bar{x}_i$ = μ_x

Figure 5.1. Sampling Distribution of the Mean, $\overline{X}_i$

we must apply a significance test, the components of which we unfold below.

To understand better how a sample statistic, such as the estimated mean, can inform us about the population, we need to consider the *sampling distribution* of the statistic. In almost every nonexperimental social science study, we in fact draw only one sample. However, statistical theory asks us to imagine that we draw a large, even infinite, number of samples, each time estimating the statistic of interest. Imagine here we draw, say, 100 simple random samples (always $N = 50$) of our students, and so get 100 estimates of the mean Library Book Return. We would not expect each estimate to be the same; sometimes the above estimate of 7 days would occur, but sometimes estimates would be higher or lower. These 100 estimates amount to scores on a variable, $\overline{X}_i$, where the subscript i indicates the particular sample.

This variable, $\overline{X}_i$, has remarkable properties. Basically, the scores, when averaged, equal the population mean, μ_X. Moreover, when plotted in a frequency distribution, they follow a normal curve. (See Figure 5.1. Along the horizontal axis the different values for the mean estimates are arrayed, along the vertical axis the frequency of each estimate.) Why is this? Because of the *central limit theorem*. It tells us mathematically that the sampling distribution of the estimated means is essentially normal, given large samples. (What is large? A common rule-of-thumb is $N > 30$.) Further, the normality of this sampling distribution holds, even if the variable on which it is estimated does not have a normal distribution in the population. For example, the variable of Library Book Return days itself need not be normal. These powerful theoretical results, when properly invoked, allow valuable use of the normality assumption for significance testing.

Besides granting that the sampling distribution of means is normal, let us add, for the moment, the assumption that the variance of the X variable and consequently its square root—the standard deviation—is known. For instance, say we know for a fact that the standard deviation of Library Book Return days in the 1st-year student population is 3. The standard deviation of the estimated means variable $\overline{X}_i$ has the following formula,

$$\text{S.D.}(\overline{X}_i) = \frac{\text{population S.D.}(X)}{\sqrt{N}} . \qquad [5.1]$$

Applying this formula to our data example, the $\text{S.D.}(\overline{X}_i) = 3/\sqrt{50} = 3/7.07 = .42$.

We now have the elements to carry out a significance test. To summarize, we have a *variable* $\overline{X}_i$, normally distributed with mean μ_X and standard deviation $\text{S.D.}(\overline{X}_i)$. As discussed in the last chapter, when a variable has a normal distribution, the probability that any score equals or exceeds +/−1.96 standard deviations from the mean is 5%, or .05. For convenience, consider the scores on $\overline{X}_i$ as standard scores, otherwise known as Z-*scores*:

$$Z = \frac{\overline{X}_i - \mu_X}{\text{S.D.}(\overline{X}_i)} . \qquad [5.2]$$

We can now say the probability that the absolute value of any Z-score is greater than or equal to 1.96 is .05. Put another way, there is only 1 chance in 20 that a sample mean exceeds by about 2 standard deviations the population mean. This benchmark helps answer the question, "Given that we observe a particular sample mean, say 7, how likely is it that the population mean is zero?"

Let us apply a "Z-test" directly to our rival hypotheses. Assuming the null hypothesis is true, then the population mean μ_X is zero. This leads to the following simplification of the above Z-score formula:

$$Z = \frac{\overline{X}_i - \mu_X}{\text{S.D.}(\overline{X}_i)} \qquad [5.3a]$$

$$= \frac{\overline{X}_i - 0}{\text{S.D.}(\overline{X}_i)} \qquad [5.3b]$$

$$= \frac{\overline{X}_i}{\text{S.D.}(\overline{X}_i)}. \qquad [5.3c]$$

If this Z for the estimated mean is greater than or equal to 1.96 in absolute value, then the probability that the population mean is zero is .05 or less. In other words, the chance of a zero population mean is so low that we reject it as a possibility. Instead, we conclude that the population mean is different from zero, at the .05 level of significance.

Applying Equation 5.3c to our Library Book Return example, $Z = 7/.42 = 16.66$. This Z-score well exceeds the cut-point of 1.96, indicating statistical significance at .05. It is highly unlikely that for the 1st-year student population the mean Library Book Return is zero. Therefore, we reject the null hypothesis and entertain the rival that, generally speaking, 1st-year students are late in returning their library books.

The only difficulty with the above conclusion of statistical significance is that the test assumes the population standard deviation of X, Library Book Returns, is known (see again the numerator of Equation 5.1). In this study, or almost any other, such an assumption is unrealistic. However, we do have at hand the sample standard deviation of X—S_X—which is 4. Fortunately, we can use this estimate, substituting it for the numerator of Equation 5.1. (The denominator remains the same, except $N - 1$ is used instead of N, in order to correct for degrees of freedom.) Given our null hypothesis of $\mu_X = 0$, the test can be simply written as follows:

$$t = \frac{\overline{X}}{S_X/\sqrt{N-1}}. \qquad [5.4]$$

Calculating this value for our example, $t = 7/(4/\sqrt{49}) = 7/(4/7) = 12.25$.

This *t-statistic*, as it is called, follows a *t*-distribution, rather than the normal, Z distribution. Fortunately, the two distributions are very similar, each bell-shaped and symmetrical. Indeed, with a large sample, they are virtually identical. However, one wrinkle, in terms of testing, is that degrees of freedom need to be taken into account, to select just the right *t*-distribution. For our case, the *t*-statistic has a *t*-distribution with $N - 1$ or 49 degrees of freedom. To carry out a significance test at the .05 level, we may refer to a *t-table* (available in the back of any statistics book) and find the critical value for a *t*-distribution with 49 degrees of freedom. Here, that critical value is 2.01. (Note how close this is to the earlier, critical value for Z, of 1.96. These critical values are virtually identical, as is expected once the sample size passes 30 or so.) If our *t*-statistic equals or exceeds the critical value, then the estimate is statistically significant at .05 or better. Because the *t*-statistic in our test surpasses the critical value ($12.25 > 2.01$), we continue to reject the null hypothesis that average Library Book Return days is zero.

Applying the Logic:
Bivariate Measures of Association

Above, the logic of significance testing has been laid bare. A statistic is calculated on a random sample and, with certain plausible assumptions about the sampling distribution of that statistic, reliable inferences are made about the population. The origins and application of the test for an elementary statistic, the mean, are now clear enough. When the sample mean registers statistically significant at .05, we reject the null hypothesis, and we know why we are doing so. The method of significance tests is the same for the bivariate statistics, although the explication can be more complicated and the distributional assumptions harder to follow. With respect to the last point, we note the binding role of the normality assumption. A test statistic may follow another distribution, such as the *t*-distribution or the chi-square, but math traces these back to the normal curve (Mohr, 1990, pp. 21-22).

This background allows a swift understanding of significance testing for the measures of association under study. First consider Pearson's *r*, with which the null of no relationship between X and Y is tested against the rival hypothesis of a relationship. More formally,

$$H_0: \rho = 0$$

$$H_1: \rho \neq 0$$

where ρ (rho) is the population correlation coefficient.

Classically, the assumption is that the sample comes out of a bivariate normal population. Then, if rho is zero, the r yields a test statistic following a t-distribution with $N - 2$ degrees of freedom. The null hypothesis is rejected when the critical t-table value is exceeded. In the case at hand, relating Parents' Education and Academic Ability, recall $r = .79$. The t-statistic accompanying this coefficient is 9.02. Consulting a t-table, the critical value for a t-distribution with 48 degrees of freedom is 2.01, assuming a .05 level of significance. Clearly, according to this test, the correlation coefficient is significant. Further, it has been shown that the test statistic for r has the same distribution, when Y is normal but X is not (see Liebetrau, 1983, pp. 47-49). Here, this means that we need not worry about the normality of X, Parents' Education. Still, the distribution in the sample suggests X is essentially normal (e.g., mean = 13.8, median = 14, mode = 12; skewness = .22). Further, as already discussed in Chapter 3, Y appears at least approximately normal. We conclude, without resort to further assumptions, that X and Y are significantly correlated. Given this sample correlation, there is less than 1 chance in 20 that Parents' Education and Academic Ability are really unrelated in the student population.

What about significance testing with our ordinal measure of association, tau-b? Unlike Pearson's r, it never depends on the assumption of a bivariate normal population. Moreover, the joint distribution of the variables need not be known. Therefore, tau-b is sometimes referred to as a "distribution-free" statistic. For large samples, $N > 30$, it has a sampling distribution close to normal (see Gibbons, 1993, pp. 2-24). Most computer statitical packages give an approximate standard error for tau-b, which can be used to calculate significance. For example, SYSTAT, on which our calculations are based, yields an asymptotic standard error (ASE) of .10 for our reported tau-b of .38. Because the tau-b estimate well exceeds twice the ASE (.38/.10 = 3.8), we can safely conclude that the coefficient is statistically significant at .05. In other words, it is fairly certain that Student Motivation and Advisor Evaluation are related to each other in the 1st-year class as a whole.

Last, consider significance testing for nominal measures of association. Assume the nominal variables are drawn in a random sample and the underlying sampling distribution is multinomial. Given the sample size is great enough, lambda as a statistic approximates a normal distribution. Further, some statistical packages, such as SYSTAT, report an asymptotic standard error (ASE) for lambda. This ASE can be used for significance testing if caution is exercised close to the extreme values of lamba, 0 or 1 (Liebetrau, 1983, pp. 19-23). Recall that, in our example, Community Type was related to Religious Affiliation, lambda = .17. For this value, ASE = .13, suggesting that the relationship is not significant at .05. That is, the coefficient is clearly less than twice its standard error, .17/.13 = 1.31. Thus we fail to reject the null hypothesis of no relationship between the two variables in the student population.

A widely used general test for whether a statistically significant relationship exists between two nominal variables is the *chi-square* test. Suppose the row variable and the column variable are unrelated or, more precisely, *independent,* in the population. Then, given a random sample of the variables, we have certain expectations about the observed cell frequencies. In general, the observed cell frequencies would reflect the underlying independence of the variables. Take, as an example, Table 4.2, relating Community Type and Religious Affilation. If Community Type is independent of Religious Affiliation, the overall proportion of community type—urban versus rural—will be reflected within each religious category. This is a "long-run" expectation (i.e., over repeated samples) but still, in our particular scientific sample, we would be surprised if the expectation were not closely met. Therefore, assuming independence, the 60%-40% (urban-rural) split should more or less reproduce itself for each religion. For instance, because there are 21 Catholics total, then $(.60 \times 21) = 12.6$, which says that about 13 of them would be expected to be urban. Similarly, for Protestants the expectation would be 12 urban (i.e., $.60 \times 20 = 12$), for Jews the expectation would be 5 urban (i.e., $.60 \times 9 = 5.4$). We actually observe 15 urban Catholics, 9 urban Protestants, and 6 urban Jews. In sum, the observed frequencies depart from the expected frequencies; the difference for Catholics is +2 (i.e., $15 - 13$), for Protestants it is -3 (i.e., $9 - 12$), for Jews it is +1 (i.e., $6 - 5$).

Are the observed frequencies far enough from the expected frequencies that we must reject the hypothesis of independence between X and Y? The *chi-square* (χ^2) test helps answer this question. If the chi-squared value, as calculated in the formula below, exceeds a critical value, we reject the independence hypothesis.

$$\chi^2 = \sum_{i=1}^{I} \sum_{k=1}^{K} \frac{(O_{ik} - E_{ik})^2}{E_{ik}} \qquad [5.5]$$

where the row variable has I categories; the column variable has K categories; (i, k) is a cell, located by the particular I and K categories; the O are the observed cell frequencies; and the E are the expected cell frequencies.

This χ^2 statistic follows the chi-square distribution with $(I - 1)(K - 1)$ degrees of freedom, assuming the variables are independent. If it surpasses a critical absolute value, as can be judged by consultation of a chi-square table (at the back of any statistics book), the hypothesis of independence is rejected. For the case at hand, $\chi^2 = 3.19$. This falls short of the critical value of 5.99 (at 2 degrees of freedom) necessary for significance at .05. We cannot reject the hypothesis of independence. As with the significance test results from the lambda, we fail to conclude that Community Type and Religion are related.

Above, we have considered significance tests appropriate to different measures of association. Although the particulars vary, according to the dictates of the level of measurement, the logic of the test is always the same. Is the relationship significant? If "yes," reject the null (and conclude there is probably a relationship). If "no," do not reject the null (and conclude there is probably not a relationship). These, of course, are the bare bones, and no such set of rules, mindlessly followed, will always suffice. The application and interpretation of significance tests requires careful judgment. Below, we cover a number of central issues with which the careful researcher must cope.

Critical Issues

When a student is initially exposed to significance testing for measures of association, some conventions may seem arbitrary. Why do we focus on rejecting the null hypothesis of a zero association when different values could be posited? One reason is that it offers a benchmark other social scientists understand and accept. Another is that we seldom agree on what those different values would be. Researcher A might insist it be .2, Researcher B might argue for .4, and Researcher C might suggest .6. After all, it is usually because we are uncertain about what the value is—and whether it is different from zero—that the research is undertaken in the first place. Convincing repeated rejections of the null hypothesis offer important cumulative evidence of the nature of the relationship between an X and a Y, and certainly, in principle, they can lead to the specification and testing of rival nonzero hypotheses.

Another perplexing issue, at least on its face, is why the level of .05 is commonly chosen. Why not select some other level, say .06? After all, a risk of being wrong 6 times out of 100 is hardly different from 5 out of 100 (as implied by the .05 level). There are at least three answers. First, classically, the significance level is set before the test is carried out. Hence, a posttest switch to .06 appears whimsical, even fraudulent. Second, the level should be readily communicable to other scholars. A setting at .06 would seem strange, as no one in social science follows that convention. Having said these things, it is possible that a finding of .06 is worth reporting. Theory, prior research, and design may all indicate that X is related to Y. In that case, the .06 may be viewed as supporting that conclusion. Of course, this deviation from the .05 convention must be defended, and the defender prepared to overcome the possible skepticism of critics.

The third answer to the question, "why .05?," is that, indeed, alternative conventions are occasionally followed. Most often, that alternative is .01. If a coefficient registers statistical significance at .01, then there is only 1 chance in 100 that X and Y are not related in the population. Thus we reject the null hypothesis with more confidence, as compared to significance at .05. More formally, the change of level from .05 to .01 reduces our risk of *Type I error*—rejection of the null even though it is true. (Under .05 we are wrong 5 times out of 100, but under .01 we are wrong only 1 time out of 100.) However, that strategy is not without its costs. Specifically, by this effort to lower the risk of Type I error we increase the risk of *Type II error*—failure to reject the null hypothesis even though it is false. (This is so because .01 sets a higher standard for rejection.) We would like to avoid both errors but cannot, as they are involved in a trade-off. Attempts to reduce one necessarily increase the other. It is perhaps not surprising, then, that the .05 level is so widely used, for its standard for rejecting the null—a risk of only 1 in 20 of being wrong—is intuitively already rather high.

Because conventional practice requires the reporting of significance tests at a fixed level, .05 (or perhaps .01), the novice may worry about the hand labor. After all, examination of several different measures of association, for different levels of measurement, in principle demands consultation of different test statistics and their respective tables, such as a t-table or a chi-square table. This can be tedious. Fortunately, however, virtually all computer statistical packages automatically provide for each measure the relevant statistic and its particular (as opposed to preset) calculated probability level. Although this is timesaving, one must be careful not to misread the numbers. A common beginner's mistake is to read "prob. = .0000" as indicating that there is no chance that rejection of the null is wrong. Instead, it really means, written out, that it is ".0001," which says there is 1 chance in 10,000 that rejection of the null is wrong. That is a low probability, but not zero, as we can never be absolutely certain of our hypothesis. Another beginner's mistake is to read a calculated probability number below .05, such as ".043," as not significant at .05. Of course it is, however, because .043 < .05. Fortunately, these careless mistakes, once corrected, are not likely to be made twice.

When analyzing the bivariate relationships in a data set we have gathered, we tend to hope we will "find significance," at least for our "pet" hypotheses. However, even with a scientifically designed study, we may not. Why? The initial response, obviously, is that our "pet" hypothesis relating, say, X and Y, was wrong. But, suppose it is not wrong. What factors might work against the finding of statistical significance, even though in the population X and Y are really related? First is Type II error, mentioned above. That is, by chance, in this particular sample, we cannot reject the null. We know, after all, that this can happen 5 times out of 100, if the level is .05. Second, the sample size may be so small (say, < 20) that it is very difficult to reject the null. Third, the magnitude of the coefficient may be small, which also makes it harder to reject the null. For example, other things being equal, a Pearson's r of .40 is more likely to register significant than a Pearson's r of .20. Fourth, the variance of X or Y (or both) may be restricted, which makes the relationship relatively difficult to detect. It is important to recognize these potential difficulties before finally drawing conclusions about an unexpectedly insignificant relationship. If any or all of these difficulties are suspected, the solution may lie in another study, perhaps with a bigger sample and a different design. Clearly, it is easier to ask for a new study than to do one. All the more reason to "do it right" in the first place.

Summary and Conclusion

In the social sciences, we almost invariably study samples, in order to infer to populations. With the goal of inference in mind, analysis of the relationship between two variables is guided by two fundamental questions: Is there a relationship? and How strong is that relationship? To help answer the first question, a significance test is applied. If the answer is "no," we tend to think there is not a relationship. If the answer is "yes," we tend to think there is a relationship. In the latter case, the second question on "strength" becomes relevant, and we answer it through evaluation of the magnitude of the appropriate measure of association, guided by the discussion of the last chapter.

6. SIMPLE REGRESSION

Most measures of association are, in fact, *nondirectional.* That is, when calculated, it is not necessary to indicate which variable is hypothesized to influence the other. Thus, for the correlation coefficient, $r_{XY} = r_{YX}$. Similarly, the tau-b calculation yields the same number regardless of which variable is labeled row and which is labeled column. In other words, the measures are symmetric. (An obvious exception is lambda, λ, which requires that one variable, say X, be designated the predictor. A formula for an asymmetric lambda does exist, but it yields a highly ambiguous interpretation.) Generally speaking, measures of association show to what degree, on a zero-to-one scale, two variables are linked. Undeniably, it is important to establish, or to reject, such links. But it is only a first step.

Take the example of the correlation ($r = .79$) between Academic Ability and Parents' Education in our Wintergreen College study. This coefficient suggests a rather strong association. However, it suggests no more, for it fails to address the structure of the relationship. Does Parents' Education influence Academic Ability, or does Academic Ability influence Parents' Education? We suppose the "causal arrow" flows essentially from Parents' Education to Academic Ability, but the "r" does not incorporate this assumption. Further, when Parents' Education varies, what exactly is the change we expect to observe in Academic Ability? Again, "r" is silent. Often, when we examine the relationship between an X and a Y, we wish to estimate directly these structural, not to say causal, connections between X and Y. When that is our purpose, then correlational analysis should be replaced by regression analysis. (For an introductory treatment of applied regression, see Lewis-Beck, 1980.)

Y as a Function of X

Suppose two variables, X and Y. Designate Y as the *dependent variable* (i.e., the "effect," or the variable to be explained). Designate X as the

TABLE 6.1
Observations From a Perfect Relationship Between X and Y

X Observations	Y Observations
0	4
1	10
2	16
3	22
4	28
5	34
$Y = 4 + 6X$	

independent variable (the "cause," or the explanatory variable). Two variables may be joined mathematically according to different functional forms. Some forms are quite complicated, as evidenced in the perusal of any physics text. Others are simple, as that underlying the data of Table 6.1, with observations on an X and a Y. Recalling elementary algebra, it is easy to show that this relationship is perfectly linear.

The general formula expressing a line is

$$Y = a + bX. \qquad [6.1]$$

A particular line is determined by the values of "a" (the *intercept*) and "b" (the *slope*). For the data of Table 6.1, the line is $Y = 4 + 6X$.

Given any X value in the table, the formula flawlessly predicts the accompanying Y value. Further, using the observations, we go on to draw the line and illustrate graphically the meanings of intercept and slope (see Figure 6.1).

Unfortunately, this example is unrealistic for social science data. Although we might expect variable X and variable Y to be related, it would not likely be perfect. Because of the complexities of the real world, we accept some error in our predictions. Thus it would be more accurate to write

$$Y = a + bX + e,$$

where e is the error term.

To illustrate, let us imagine that the values of Table 6.1 actually come from a population of parents in a community, with X = number of children and Y = annual contribution in dollars to the school fall fund-raiser. We

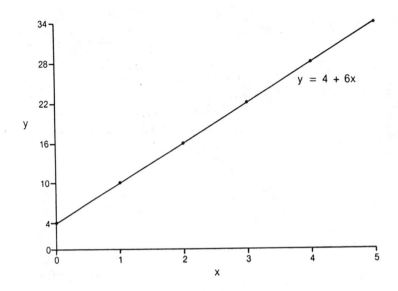

Figure 6.1. Perfect Linear Relationship Between X and Y

anticipate those with more children will contribute more money; however, we do not count on the relationship being totally predictive. For instance, some parents of large families will contribute less than expected, others even more. After all, it is not surprising that the variable, number of children, is not the sole determinant of contributions. In Figure 6.2, we see a more realistic scatterplot, with more observations on X (number of children) and Y (school fund contributions).

Visually, the relationship still appears basically linear. Our eyes are pulled up a slope through the points, as they sweep left to right. But what is the precise line? Is it still $Y = 4 + 6X$, which we have taken the liberty of sketching in as line 1? Or does another line actually fit better? Two alternative lines are sketched besides: $Y = 2 + 7X$ (labeled line 2), and $Y = 5 + 5X$ (labeled line 3). Perhaps one of them is preferred. To decide which, of all possible lines, is "best," we resort to the *least squares principle*.

The Least Squares Principle

The best line generates the least prediction error. But how to define prediction error? For an individual case, first think of prediction error as

44

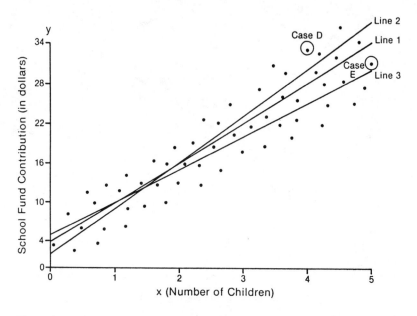

Figure 6.2. Possible Linear Relationships Between X (Number of Children) and Y (School Fund Contributions)

the difference between the observed value (Y_i) and the value predicted by the line ($\hat{Y}_i$). (The $\hat{}$, the "hat," over the value indicates a predicted value). Take Case D in Figure 6.2, with $X = 4$. Line 1 yields $\hat{Y} = 28$, but $Y = 33$, for an individual prediction error of +5. Now take Case E, with $X = 5$. Line 1 yields $\hat{Y}_i = 34$, but $Y = 31$, for an individual prediction error of −3. Likewise, for each case, individual prediction errors could be calculated.

What is the total prediction error for the line? Initially, the temptation is to add up the individual prediction errors. But that temptation is to be avoided, for the positive and negative errors tend to cancel each other. (For example, just adding the individual errors on Case D and Case E, +5 − 3 = +2. Obviously, this is a misleadingly low number.) To solve the problem of the signs canceling, we could use absolute values of all the individual prediction errors, or square them. The latter is favored, because it allows a more powerful mathematics of inference. Hence, the total prediction error of a line comes to be defined as the sum of the squares of the individual errors, written

$$\text{SSE} = \sum (Y_i - \hat{Y}_i)^2 .$$

An SSE could be calculated for line 1, and also calculated for line 2 and line 3. Comparing the three sums, we could then select which of these lines was better, in terms of yielding a smaller value. Still, that selection, say it was line 2, would not necessarily be the "best" one out of all possible lines. Another line—a line 4, or a line 5, and so on ad infinitum—might be tried, and perhaps found to yield yet a better fit. Fortunately, there is a way out of this dilemma. As can be demonstrated by the calculus, the following formulas provide the unique values of a and b that minimize the SSE.

$$b = \frac{\sum (X_i - \overline{X})(Y_i - \overline{Y})}{\sum (X_i - \overline{X})^2}$$

$$a = \overline{Y} - b\overline{X} .$$

These slope and intercept values are known as the *least squares* estimates. They identify a line that guarantees that the sum of the squared errors will be as small as possible, that is, "least." Below, we apply the least squares principle in order to find the best-fitting line for relating two variables in our Wintergreen College study.

Intercept and Slope

We now argue explicitly that Academic Ability is a linear function of Parents' Education. Our theoretical *model,* which also takes into account the error, is written as follows:

$$Y = a + bX + e \qquad [6.2]$$

where Y is Academic Ability exam score, X is Parents' Education, e is the error term, a is the intercept, and b is the slope.

We wish to estimate the intercept (a) and the slope (b) by using the formulas provided above. This process is called ordinary least squares (OLS) regression. Because there are two variables, we execute a *bivariate,* or *simple, regression.* However, an essential preliminary is examination of the scatterplot. Recall that in Figure 4.1, variable Y was plotted against

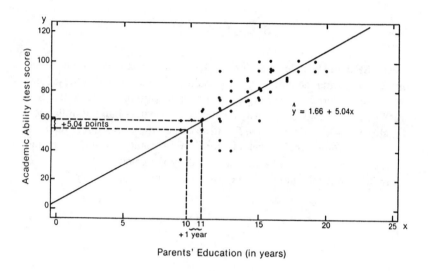

Figure 6.3. OLS Regression Line of Parents' Education (X) on Academic Ability (Y)

variable X. Visual inspection of that plot suggests the relationship is linear. The particular line is given by OLS. When we "regress" Y on X, we obtain,

$$\hat{Y} = 1.66 + 5.04X \qquad [6.3]$$

where $\hat{Y}$ is the predicted Y, 1.66 is the least squares estimate of the intercept, and 5.04 is the least squares estimate of the slope. This line is fitted to the scatterplot in Figure 6.3. Clearly, the line tracks the points, although not perfectly. Nevertheless, it is the best-fitting line possible.

How do we interpret its coefficients? First, the intercept is a constant, the value at which the line cuts the Y axis. Mathematically, it gives *the expected value for Y when X = 0.* Substantively, that suggests that when the parents had no formal education, the student could expect to miss almost every question on the entrance exam (i.e., $\hat{Y} = 1.66 + 5.04[0] = 1.66$ items correct out of 100 items). Although the intercept has an indispensable mathematical role, it may not contribute substantively to a particular analysis. Here it is not totally without sense (as it would be, for example, if it had a negative sign). After all, it is highly plausible for a student to perform very poorly in college if neither parent has ever been to school.

However, this interpretation is still risky, because it goes beyond our realm of experience. Specifically, no one in the study has a Parents' Education score lower than 9 years. In general, prediction based on values outside the known range of X values in the data set should be avoided.

The slope indicates *the expected change in Y for a unit change in X.* In the case at hand students will earn, on average, 5.04 more points on the exam for every additional year of parents' education (this is shown graphically in Figure 6.3). The slope, then, measures the effect of the independent variable. Substantively, the effect of parents' education seems rather important. For instance, when students have parents with a high score, say $X = 20$, they can expect to do much better than when parents have a low score, say $X = 10$. More precisely, the first group can expect to score about 50 points higher than the second group (i.e., $[20 - 10] \times 5.04 = 50.4$).

Prediction and Goodness-of-Fit

A simple regression equation can be used to predict Y, for a given X value. Suppose that we know a student in our study has parents with an average of 13 years of education, and we wish to predict exam performance. It is an easy thing to plug in that number and generate the prediction:

$$\hat{Y} = 1.66 + 5.04X$$

$$= 1.66 + 5.04(13)$$

$$= 1.66 + 65.52$$

$$= 67.18 .$$

[6.4]

Thus for 13 years of parents' education, we predict an exam score of about 67 items correct. Of course, it would be possible to use the equation to predict each student's performance. As can be observed in Figure 6.3, some of these predictions would be exactly right (i.e., on the line) but others would contain error (be a distance from the line). Obviously, it would be useful to have a summary measure of how well the prediction equation performs. The leading measure for that is the R-squared, R^2, also known as the *coefficient of determination,* described below.

First, imagine that you want to predict each Y score but you only know their mean value, $\bar{Y}$. In that situation, the best guess will be $\bar{Y}$. Not surprisingly, most of these mean guesses will deviate substantially from the observed values. We summarize these deviations as follows (squaring them to avoid the problem of signs cancelling):

$$\text{Total sum of squared deviations (TSS)} = \sum(Y_i - \bar{Y}_i)^2. \qquad [6.5]$$

Fortunately, we know more than $\bar{Y}$. Presumably, at least some of this deviation from the mean can be accounted for, given that the regression prediction $\hat{Y}$ is known. We summarize the deviations accounted for by the regression as follows:

$$\text{Regression sum of squared deviations (RSS)} = \sum(\hat{Y}_i - \bar{Y}_i)^2. \qquad [6.6]$$

If the regression fails to account for all the deviation from the mean, then error will remain, summarized as

$$\text{Error sum of squared deviations (ESS)} = \sum(Y_i - \hat{Y}_i)^2. \qquad [6.7]$$

Thus we see that the variation in the dependent variable, Y, defined as TSS, has two components—one accounted for by the regression (RSS), the other not accounted for (ESS). The formula for the R-squared is simply,

$$R^2 = \text{RSS/TSS}. \qquad [6.8]$$

On one hand, when the regression accounts for all the variation, then R-squared = 1.0, indicating a perfect linear fit. On the other hand, when R-squared = .00, then there is no linear relationship between X and Y. Usually, *goodness-of-fit*, as measured by the R^2, falls between these extreme values. In our example, $R^2 = .63$. This says that Parents' Education accounts for 63% of the variation in Academic Ability, according to the linear model. Depending on our theoretical confidence in the model, we may go on to assert that Parents' Education "explains" 63% of the variation in Academic Ability. (The word "explains" is in quotation marks, to warn the reader that what may appear a good statistical explanation is not necessarily a good, or complete, theoretical explanation. Generally speaking, when researchers use the word "explanation" without modifiers, they are presumed to be discussing theory.)

Another measure of goodness-of-fit that is sometimes used is the *standard error of estimate* (SEE) of Y. For a simple regression, it is calculated as follows:

$$ \text{SEE} = \sqrt{\frac{\sum (Y_i - \hat{Y}_i)^2}{N-2}} . \qquad [6.9] $$

We see that the formulation provides something close to an average prediction error for a model. (It will always be somewhat larger in magnitude than the APE, average absolute prediction error $[\sum |Y_i - \hat{Y}_i|/N]$. However, this difference between SEE and APE diminishes with increasing sample size, as contemplation of the above denominator makes evident.) When prediction is without error, SEE = 0. In the case at hand, SEE = 10.7 exam items, suggesting that on average the model generates a fair amount of prediction error. If the researcher's goal is merely to predict test outcomes, this indicates that the equation will not do strikingly well.

When using SEE to assess overall model quality, it can be difficult to pass precise judgment, because the measure has no theoretical upper bound. That is, as error increases, the magnitude of SEE always grows larger. This contrasts with the R^2, which is bounded at both ends (1= perfect linearity, 0 = no linearity). Because of this "boundary issue," the R^2 may be preferred over the SEE when one wishes to assess goodness-of-fit.

Significance Tests and Confidence Intervals

In regression analysis, we almost always apply least squares to sample data, with a sample equation such as

$$ Y = a + bX + e . \qquad [6.10] $$

However, the goal is inference to population parameters. Customarily, we distinguish the population equation by the use of Greek letters,

$$ Y = \alpha + \beta X + \epsilon \qquad [6.11] $$

where α (alpha) is the population intercept, β (beta) is the population slope, and ϵ is the error term.

A vital question is whether the estimate of the population parameter is statistically significant. The logic of significance testing, already discussed, easily extends to regression. Can the null hypothesis—no relationship in the population—be rejected? Consider rival hypotheses for the slope:

$$H_0: \beta = 0$$

$$H_1: \beta \neq 0$$

A test using the t-distribution is preferred, because we do not know the standard deviation of the slope but rather have to estimate it from the sample. The test statistic can be written

$$t_{N-2} = \frac{b - \beta}{S_b} \qquad [6.12]$$

where $N - 2$ is the number of degrees of freedom; b is the estimated slope; β is the population slope; and S_b is the estimated standard deviation of the slope, called the *standard error*, calculated as follows:

$$S_b = \sqrt{\frac{\sum(Y - \hat{Y})^2/(N - 2)}{\sum(X - \bar{X})^2}} \ .$$

Given the null hypothesis that the population slope equals zero, this t-statistic simplifies to

$$t_{N-2} = \frac{b - 0}{S_b} \qquad [6.13]$$

$$= \frac{b}{S_b} \ . \qquad [6.14]$$

Let us apply the test at the .05 level of statistical significance, for our particular data example from Wintergreen College above, where $b = 5.04$. Is this coefficient statistically significant? Consulting a t-table, we find that, given 48 degrees of freedom ($N - 2 = 48$), the critical t-value is 2.01. Our actual t-score, 9.02 (i.e., 5.04/.56), far exceeds the critical cutoff. We reject the null hypothesis and conclude that it is highly likely that Parents' Education is related to Academic Ability in the student population.

The above result conforms to a convenient rule-of-thumb: *When the t-ratio (b/S_b) is greater than or equal to 2.00 in absolute value, the coefficient is almost certainly significant at .05.* This handy rule is quickly accepted after study of the t-table. For a sample of infinite size, the critical t-value is 1.96. Further, this critical value for t does not noticeably exceed 2 until samples become very small. To take examples, with a sample of 30 the critical t is only 2.04, and with a sample of 10 it is 2.23. It is no wonder that busy researchers, when perusing pages of printout and many regression equations, employ this rule-of-thumb to arrive at preliminary judgments about the relevance of findings.

The above rules for significance testing also apply to the other parameter we are estimating—the intercept. For these data, the intercept estimate has a t-ratio of $a/S_a = .21$. At a glance, we recognize that this number is far below the threshold critical value of 2.00. We immediately conclude that the intercept estimate, $a = 1.66$, is not statistically significant at .05. The implication is that, in the population, the intercept may well be zero.

With significance testing, we set up a standard for rejecting the hypothesis that a coefficient is zero. But if it is not zero, what is it likely to be? Return to consideration of that more interesting parameter—the slope. Of course, the most likely answer is the *point estimate* itself—b. However, it would be foolish to assert blindly that the point estimate is exactly right. Perhaps it is a little less than the population parameter, perhaps a little more. To entertain this possibility, an *interval estimate, called a confidence interval,* can be constructed. A nondirectional (called a *two-tail*), 95% confidence interval for the above slope is calculated as follows:

$$b = \pm (T_c)(S_b)$$

where b, S_b are defined as before. The term T_c is the critical t-value needed, given a two-tail, 95% confidence interval test. This critical t-value is necessarily the same as that for the .05 statistical significance test, with the same number of tails. (The statistical significance test implied by a given confidence interval is found by subtracting the latter from 1, for example, $1 - .95 = .05$.) Here is the two-tailed, 95% confidence interval for our above Wintergreen College example:

$$5.04 \pm 2.01(.56).$$

On the basis of these estimates, we are 95% confident that the population slope lies between 3.91 and 6.17. The value of zero does not fall within the range (something we knew automatically having already established it was significant at .05). Further, in this case, the range of values is fairly tight, about 4 to 6. Even accepting the lowest number as correct, there is a strong implication that Parents' Education has a big impact.

All of our hypothesis tests, until now, have been nondirectional, or two-tailed. That is, the alternative hypothesis has argued X is related to Y but does not say whether that relationship is positive or negative. Obviously, though, sometimes we believe the alternative hypothesis carries a particular sign. In the case at hand, for instance, we would hardly expect a negative sign, indicating that greater Parents' Education produced lower Academic Ability test scores. It would seem efficient to incorporate this prior knowledge, formulating a one-directional, or one-tail, hypothesis test; thus

$$H_0: \beta = 0$$

$$H_1: \beta > 0.$$

Here is the one-tailed, 95% confidence interval, for these data:

$$\beta > [b - (T_c)(S_b)] \qquad [6.15]$$

where the definitions are the same as before, but note that T_c, the critical value, must now be different, given the test is one-tail. Hence,

$$\beta > [5.04 - (1.68)(.56)] = 5.04 - .94 = 4.1.$$

This value, which represents the low end of the band, is far from zero. At 95% confidence, we reject the null and conclude that Parents' Education is most likely positively related to Academic Ability. Further, differing from the earlier two-tailed estimate, we believe that it is not likely to be lower in its effect than 4.1. Thus by incorporating prior knowledge we get closer to the real boundary for the effect.

Presenting Regression Results:
A Summary Guide

In this chapter, the fundamental bits and pieces of regression analysis have been explicated. The calculations on the computer printout are no longer strange numbers. But how to move from the printout to the page? Regression results should be presented clearly and comprehensively. The following format, which we review with the Wintergreen College example, has much to recommend it:

$$Y = 1.66 + 5.04*X + e$$

$$(.21) \quad (9.02)$$

$$R^2 = .63 \quad N = 50 \quad SEE = 10.72$$

where Y is the Academic Ability test score (in number of items correct), X is Parents' Education (in years), e is the error term, the figures in parentheses are t-ratios, * indicates statistical significance at the .05 level (two-tail), R^2 is the coefficient of determination, N is the sample size (number of students), and SEE is the standard error of estimate of Y.

When the regression results are so presented in this "box," the reader has readily available much that is needed to evaluate the analysis— variables, measures, coefficients, significance tests, goodness-of-fit, and sample information. The conscientious researcher will use this format, or one similar to it, when writing up regression findings.

7. MULTIPLE REGRESSION

With *multiple regression,* we include more than one independent variable. There are two basic reasons why this might be desirable. First, we suppose that the dependent variable, Y, is influenced by more than one thing. Second, we want to increase our confidence that, indeed, a particular X influences Y, after other things are taken into account. The general model is written as follows:

$$Y = a + b_1X_1 + b_2X_2 + b_3X_3 \ldots b_kX_k + e \qquad [7.1]$$

54

where Y is the dependent variable; X_1, X_2, X_3, ..., X_k are independent variables; a is the estimated intercept; b_1, b_2, b_3, ..., b_k are estimated partial slopes; and e is the error term.

According to the model, Y is a linear additive function of multiple variables. Estimates for the coefficients are arrived at through application of the least squares principle. The calculus gives the unique combination of $a, b_1, b_2, b_3, ..., b_k$ values that minimizes the sum of the squared errors, providing the best linear fit. However, that fit is not a line to be drawn on a two-dimensional space, as in a simple regression. Consider the elementary case of two independent variables. Least squares finds the plane that best fits a cluster of points in three-dimensional space. When there are more than three independent variables, the plane becomes a hyperplane, fitted in $(k + 1)$ dimensions.

Interpretation of the coefficients involves straightforward extensions from simple regression. The intercept estimate indicates the expected value of Y, *when all the X are zero*. A partial slope estimate, b_k, indicates the expected change in Y for a unit change in X_k, *with all the other X held constant*. An application of these interpretations, along with their supporting statistics, is given below. (For a more extended treatment of multiple regression, consult Berry & Feldman, 1985.)

An Example

In our Wintergreen College study, it is unrealistic to believe that entrance exam scores are influenced solely by parents' education. Obviously, many other things can affect student performance. One such variable, already measured in our study (see Table 2.1), is type of community. Although we may be wrong, we suspect that students from smaller communities do better than urbanites. Let us hypothesize that, in addition to Parents' Education, this second variable makes a difference. This suggests the following multiple regression model:

$$Y = a + b_1X_1 + b_2X_2 + e \qquad [7.2]$$

where Y is the Academic Ability exam score (items correct), X_1 is Parents' Education (average in years), and X_2 is Community Type (0 = urban, 1 = rural).

Ordinary least squares (OLS) estimates for the model are

$$Y = 5.46 + 4.44*X_1 + 11.28*X_2 + e$$

$$(.79) \quad (8.69) \quad (3.99) \qquad [7.3]$$

$$R^2 = .72 \quad N = 50 \quad SEE = 9.36$$

where the variables are defined as above; the figures in parentheses are t-ratios; * indicates statistical significance at .05, two-tail; N is the sample size; SEE is the standard error of estimate for Y; and R^2 is the *coefficient of multiple determination.*

These results are informative. The coefficient for Community Type, $b_2 = 11.28$, has a t-ratio well beyond the still applicable rule-of-thumb cutoff ($t = |2.00|$) for statistical significance at .05, two-tail. Almost certainly, the variable makes a difference. The slope estimates that, once X_1 is held constant, rural residents can expect an exam score about 11 points higher than urban residents. That impact, although not overwhelming, is certainly not small. Further, Parents' Education (X_1) registers a statistically significant effect. According to this multiple regression estimate, an additional year of Parents' Education produces an expected increase in the Academic Ability score of 4.44 points. This estimate is slightly lower than that for the bivariate regression (at 5.04); nevertheless, it is more accurate because of the control introduced by holding X_2 constant. Overall, this multivariate model offers a better fit than the bivariate model, showing an increase in R^2 of .09 (from .63 to .72). As well, the SEE demonstrates improvement, shrinking from 10.71 earlier to 9.36 here. Statistically, as well as theoretically, the model appears to be a step forward.

The Notion of Statistical Control

In multiple regression analysis, it is extremely important to understand how *statistical control* works. To understand it better, we first contrast it with *experimental control.* Does X influence Y? In experimental research, we try to answer this query by manipulating X, *after the subjects have been randomly assigned to groups* for receiving the X "treatment." Take a basic example from a grade school math class. The teacher, Janet Brown, is introducing the metric system and wants to know whether the students learn better from a lecture or from reading about it on their own. The "treatment," or independent variable, becomes Instructional Method (X_1), and has two values, scored 1 = lecture, 0 = reading on their own. The dependent variable, Metric System Knowledge (Y), will be scored on a 20-item quiz. She randomly assigns the 50 students to treatment groups, half to one type of instruction, half to the other. After marking the quizzes, she performs a significance test, finding that the average quiz scores for the two groups are significantly different at .05. (A simple regression analysis, with an examination of the t-ratio, might be the basis for this assessment. Although experimental data are traditionally analyzed with analysis of variance, regression analysis may yield highly similar, even identical, statistical results. See Iversen & Norpoth, 1987.)

Ms. Brown goes on to conclude that Instructional Method caused the difference. Of course, she cannot be absolutely certain of her conclusion, but she is in a position of "strong inference" because she has ruled out, with a high degree of probability, the possibility that other independent variables ($X_2, \ldots, X_k$) caused the difference between the two groups. Because the students were randomly assigned, there is no reason to believe that the groups differ from each other in any important way, except for the treatment. So, if their quiz scores differ significantly, we rather easily accept the argument that the manipulation of the independent variable produced it.

The situation of experimental control, with its strong inference, contrasts sharply with the statistical control afforded by multiple regression analysis. For observational data, manipulation of the values of the independent variable is usually out of the question. In any case, social, political, or psychological factors under study are virtually always beyond the direct influence of researchers themselves. With regard to our example of Metric System Knowledge (Y), a plausible nonexperimental counterpart might be that, across different grade classrooms, we observe that teachers vary in X_1, their instructional method (i.e., some lecture, some assign readings). If we then record a statistically significant relationship between X_1 and Y, the problem becomes one of sorting out whether it was the instructional method that produced it, or some other variable such as X_2. Say X_2 is room assignment, based on math aptitude. It may be that the students in the "high math aptitude rooms" are taught by the lecture method, thereby creating a correlation between Y and X_1 that is *spurious,* that is, not causal. To test this possibility of spuriousness, we could regress Y on X_1, while holding X_2 constant.

The above multiple regression equation from the Wintergreen study can actually be viewed as a test of the *spuriousness hypothesis.* One might argue that the observed bivariate relationship between Parents' Education (Y) and Academic Ability (X_1) is spurious, a product of the common influence of Community Type, X_2. That is, Community Type might determine Parents' Education, as well as Academic Ability. Then, because of common variation, X_1 would be observed related to Y, even though they were not causally linked. The above OLS results allow us to reject the hypothesis of total spuriousness. Even holding constant X_2, we see that X_1 continues to exhibit a strong effect on Y. However, the diminution of the coefficient (from 5.04 in the bivariate case to 4.44 in the multivariate case) suggests some partial, if mild, spuriousness in the original bivariate regression. Of course, that is merely another way of concluding that the slope from the multiple regression is closer to the truth, as we would expect.

Clearly, to establish the effect of a particular independent variable in a nonexperimental setting, it is important to "hold other variables constant." But in a technical sense, how does multiple regression do this? We generalize from the elementary case, Y as a function of two independent variables, X_1 and X_2. The partial regression slope of, say, X_1 can be calculated in terms of components of variation linearly unrelated to X_2:

$$b_1 = \frac{\sum(X_1 - \hat{X}_1)(Y - \hat{Y})}{\sum(X_1 - \hat{X}_1)^2} \qquad [7.4]$$

where Y is the dependent variable; X_1, X_2 are the independent variables; $\hat{X}_1 = f_1 + f_2 X_2$ (the prediction from a simple regression of X_1 on X_2); and $\hat{Y} = g_1 + g_2 X_2$ (the prediction from a simple regression of Y on X_2).

From this formulation, it is clear that the partial slope, b_1, is based on variation in X_1 and Y independent of X_2. In this way, the potential distortion from X_2 is controlled for. We say we are "holding constant" X_2 because its values no longer have anything to do with the link between X_1 and Y. Thus an increase in 1 year of Parents' Education is expected to yield a 4.44 point increase in Academic Ability, independent of the student's Community Type. Similarly, the impact of Community Type itself (as estimated by b_2) is entirely separate from the effect of X_1.

Specification Error

Before investing much faith in the validity of our least squares estimates, we need to be convinced of the essential correctness of our theoretical model. The variable Y must actually depend on the independent Xs we have included, otherwise we commit a kind of *specification error*. Put another way, do we have the "right" variables in the model? Theory and prior research are critical guides, besides the statistical results themselves. In the above model, Parents' Education and Community Type have been included on all these grounds. However, even if they belong, they are surely not the only influential variables. Should other factors be brought in? Generally, to answer such a question, a series of issues must be addressed. Does careful theorizing suggest other relevant independent variables? What does the empirical literature show? If other variables might be needed, are they measured? Measured or not, what is the cost of not including them?

Let us look again at our example. Upon reflection, it would seem that other variables might shape Academic Ability, in addition to those identified thus far. Our candidate, among variables we have measured, is Student Motivation (see Table 2.1). The more hardworking the students say they are, the better we would expect them to do on the entrance exam. (This notion receives preliminary support from examination of the correlation between the two variables, $r = .46$.) Suppose we revise our theoretical model, as follows:

$$Y = a + b_1 X_1 + b_2 X_2 + b_3 X_3 + e \qquad [7.5]$$

where Y is Academic Ability, X_1 is Parents' Education, X_2 is Community Type, and X_3 is Student Motivation.

The OLS estimates for the revised model are as follows:

$$\hat{Y} = 5.4 + 4.46 * X_1 + 11.30 * X_2 - .10 X_3$$

$$(.74) \quad (7.63) \qquad (3.88) \qquad (-.05) \qquad\qquad [7.6]$$

$$R^2 = .72 \qquad N = 50 \qquad SEE = 9.46$$

where Y, X_1, and X_2 are measured as before; X_3 is Student Motivation, scored as in Table 2.1 from low to high on a 3-point scale (0, 1, 2); and the statistics and coefficients are defined as before.

These results have much interest. The argument that Student Motivation improves entrance exam performance is not supported. The coefficient for X_3 is in fact mildly negative and far from statistical significance. (The t-ratio itself is only .05 in absolute value, a raw number not to be confused with the statistical significance level of .05, which we know requires an absolute critical value of about 2.00.) Further, the coefficients for the other variables, and the accompanying statistics, remain virtually unchanged from the two-independent-variable model. Hence, the continued omission of X_3 receives some support. Further, the original X_1 and X_2 specification sustains itself empirically, even if a possible alternative indirect measure of motivation, X_3'—Advisor Evaluation (see variable AE in Table 2.1)—is substituted. (That is, b_1 and b_2 estimates remain virtually unchanged, whereas the slope estimate b_3' falls well short of statistical significance at .05. The full equation results are not shown but readers can quickly recover them by their own analysis of the data of Table 2.1.)

Our belief is that the original X_1 and X_2 model is "true," at least as far is it goes. This belief has met the challenge of inclusion from other measured variables—X_3 and X_3'. But what about the possible independent variables that we did not measure? For instance, there may be relevant factors from the students' high school experience, such as Senior Year Grade Point Average (X_4), or Class Attendance (X_5). Take first the X_4 variable. Perhaps we should have measured X_4 but we did not. How serious is this omission from our model of Academic Ability? More precisely, what does it do to the quality of the slope estimates that we did obtain? Because X_4 is not included, it is represented only in the error term of the equation. It may be likely that the Senior Year GPA variable (X_4) would influence college Academic Ability (Y) and would also be correlated with Parents' Education (X_1). Given that situation, the b_1 estimate of the original multiple regression would be *biased* (in this case, almost certainly too large a number), because the situation violates the regression assumption that the error term be uncorrelated with the independent variables of the model. (For a summary discussion of all the regression assumptions necessary for unbiased estimation, including more discussion of desirable estimator properties, see the Appendix.)

The obvious remedy, which would not be hard to implement in the project at hand, is to measure the missing variable, X_4—Senior Year GPA—and include it in a revised estimation model. Of course, it is not always possible to measure the missing variable. In such a circumstance, much may still be salvaged. Upon serious consideration, it could be realized that the missing variable—say now it is not X_4 but rather X_5 (Class Attendance)—neither influences Y nor is correlated with the independent variables already included. (*Both* conditions are required to induce bias.) Thus X_5—and any other variable with similar characteristics—can be excluded without biasing the coefficients of the variables currently in the model. This is a fortunate theoretical condition. In an important practical sense, it means that the researcher need not introduce every potential independent variable under the sun in order to get desirable parameter estimates. *What counts is that the variables in the model should be included theoretically, and that the exclusions are not correlated with the inclusions.*

Dummy Variables

Regression analysis assumes that the variables are measured quantitatively. However, the three-independent-variable model estimated above contained X_3, an ordinal variable on Student Motivation. Technically speaking, that equation inappropriately imposes a quantitative assumption on X_3. Although this is a frequent research practice it may be that, because of it, the conclusion of a spurious relationship between X_3 and Y is erroneous. A way to overcome this measurement level violation, a solution generally applicable when the independent variables are ordinal or nominal, is *dummy variables.* To create them, one "dummies up" the G categories of the conceptual qualitative variable into $G - 1$ dummy variables.

For example, in the above case, the *conceptual variable* is ordinal—Student Motivation (originally scored 0, 1, 2). Accordingly, it has three categories ($G = 3$). Before constructing the dummies, a baseline category must be chosen. Mathematically, the baseline makes no difference, but some allow for more straightforward substantive interpretation (because the intercept estimate effectively becomes that for the baseline category). Customarily, an extreme value (here 0 or 2) is selected. Let us say "0"—the least motivated—serves. The requirement is $(G - 1) = 2$ dummies, labeled here D_1 and D_2, with the following recoding of X_3:

$$D_1 = \begin{cases} 0 & \text{if } X_3 = 0 \text{ or } 2 \\ 1 & \text{if } X_3 = 1 \end{cases}$$

$$D_2 = \begin{cases} 0 & \text{if } X_3 = 0 \text{ or } 1 \\ 1 & \text{if } X_3 = 2 . \end{cases}$$

Thus D_1 and D_2 are two quantitative, dichotomous variables, scored 0 or 1. Further, knowing a student's score on D_1 and D_2, we necessarily know which of the three categories of the conceptual variable the student placed in. For example, if $D_1 = 0$ and $D_2 = 0$, then the student must be in the "low" motivation category. (If G dummies were mistakenly constructed, say here there was an addition of D_3 to D_1 and D_2, estimation could not proceed because of the mathematical redundancy. This "dummy variable trap" is to be avoided.)

On the basis of the foregoing, we utilize quantitative dummy variables to measure Student Motivation and reestimate (OLS) the revised multiple regression as follows:

$$Y = 6.35 + 4.58 * X_1 + 11.64 * X_2 - 5.85D_1 - 1.00D_2 + e$$

$$(.90) \quad (8.07) \quad (4.12) \quad (-1.67) \quad (-.24) \qquad [7.7]$$

$$R^2 = .75 \quad \text{Adjusted } R^2 = .72 \quad N = 50 \quad \text{SEE} = 9.16$$

where Y, X_1, X_2, and the statistics are defined as before; D_1 and D_2 are the above defined dummy variables; and Adjusted R^2 is the coefficient of multiple determination, adjusted to take into account the degrees of freedom used up by adding more independent variables.

These results suggest that increases in Student Motivation, whether from low to middle (see the D_1 coefficient) or from low to high (see the D_2 coefficient), does not have a statistically significant effect on Academic Ability. (Observe their t-ratios are not close to 2.00 in absolute value.) Indeed, as when the variable was measured ordinally in the earlier equation, the sign of the relationship is mildly negative. We conclude, but with more confidence because of meeting strict measurement assumptions, that Student Motivation does not influence Academic Ability. Moreover, we see that, despite the addition of an extra variable (here we have four independent variables whereas before we had three in Equation 7.6), the R^2 does not really change after adjustment to compensate for using up more degrees of freedom. (See the adjusted R-squared reported above. For every extra independent variable added to a regression equation, one more degree of freedom is used. That means that the unadjusted R-squared, by itself, has a bit more advantage, from chance alone, of producing a higher fit. The adjusted R-squared reduces it downward, to correct for this chance advantage. When the analyst has many independent variables, and not so many cases, it is an especially good idea to report the adjusted R-squared.)

Dummy variable multiple regression, as it is sometimes called, allows tremendous analysis flexibility. (For a detailed explanation of regression with dummy variables, see Hardy, 1993.) Therefore, independent variables, regardless of their measurement level, can readily be incorporated into our quantitative models. (When the dependent variable is a dummy, hence dichotomous, OLS can still perform as an unbiased estimator but loses in efficiency. See further discussion in the Appendix.)

Collinearity

The independent variables in a nonexperimental regression analysis of sample observations are invariably *collinear.* That is, each X will be to some extent linearly related to the other Xs, singly or in combination. (For example, in the two-independent-variable model of Equation 7.3, that relationship is measured simply by the correlation between X_1 and X_2, $r =$ .30.) Because collinearity is inevitable, a little is not a problem but a lot can be. *High collinearity* tends to be problematic, because it generates very unstable slope estimates. It may render the coefficient value very uncertain. Indeed, when the instability becomes great enough, the estimated slope coefficient of an X may register statistical insignificance, when in fact this X influences Y in the population. In research practice, that is the great difficulty caused by high collinearity—the conclusion of no statistical significance despite an underlying structural link.

High collinearity tends to create large standard errors for the slope estimates. These large standard errors make for wide confidence intervals and much uncertainty over the precise slope value. Recall the formula for a 95%, two-tailed confidence interval for b:

$$b \pm (T_c)(S_b) \qquad [7.8]$$

where b is the slope estimate, T_c is the critical t-value, and S_b is the standard error of estimate of b.

Reflecting on the formula, obviously, as S_b increases, the interval around b widens, making us less sure of the value of the population slope. Indeed, when S_b becomes great enough, it becomes extremely difficult to even reject the null and assert that the population slope is anything other than zero. Put another way, declaring the slope estimate statistically significant becomes almost impossible. We see this last problem clearly after thinking again about the formula for the t-ratio used in significance testing of a slope estimate:

$$t = \frac{b}{S_b} \qquad [7.9]$$

where t is the t-ratio, b is the slope estimate, and S_b is the standard error of b.

Remembering our rule-of-thumb, as the t-ratio exceeds the absolute value of 2.00, the coefficient generally exceeds statistical significance at .05. Clearly, it becomes more difficult for t to exceed 2.00 as the denominator, S_b, becomes a bigger number. What makes S_b bigger? In other words, what increases the estimated variation of the slope? Look at this formula for the variance of a slope estimate, b_j:

$$\text{Variance } b_j = S_{b_j}^2 = \frac{S_u^2}{V_j^2} \qquad [7.10]$$

where $S_{b_j}^2$ is the estimated standard error squared of slope b_j; S_u^2 is the variance of the regression error term; and $V_j^2 = (X_j - \hat{X}_j)^2$, where $(X_j - \hat{X}_j)$ is the prediction error, or residual, from the regression of independent variable X_j on the other independent variables in the model $(X_i, i \neq j)$.

As can be seen, the variance of b_j, and thus its standard error, will become large when the denominator—V_j^2—becomes small. This denominator becomes small when the other independent variables—the X_i $(i \neq j)$— are highly predictive of X_j; that is, under the circumstance of high collinearity. This denominator also suggests a method for assessing the level of collinearity in a system, which we apply below.

When perusing regression results, the research worker should be alert to symptoms suggestive of a high collinearity problem. Are the estimates of more or less the expected magnitude? Are the signs "right"? Are the standard errors of the slopes unusually large? Is the R^2 high but the coefficients insignificant? None of these symptoms (except perhaps the last) is definitive, but their appearance should signal the beginning of a serious attempt to rule out the hypothesis that the estimates suffer from severe collinearity.

Do the symptoms of a high collinearity problem appear in the analysis of the Wintergreen College data? For heuristic purposes, reconsider the four-independent-variable model just presented above (see Equation 7.7). The estimates for the effects of Parents' Education (X_1) and Community Type (X_2) do not appear unusual in magnitude, nor are the signs unexpected. The standard error of the coefficient of X_1 does not appear especially large, although that of X_2 could not be called small. The R^2 is fairly high, but only two of the four coefficients are not significant (those of the dummy variables, D_1 and D_2). On the whole, then, the results are absent of worrisome symptoms.

Our temptation is to declare that there is no collinearity problem. However, a critic may argue that, in fact, the coefficients of D_1 and D_2 are failing to register statistical significance simply because of the large amount of collinearity in the system (and not, say, because D_1 and D_2 really do not have anything to do with Y in the population). At this point, a direct assessment of collinearity levels is recommended, and that is done by regressing each X_j on all the other X_i ($i \neq j$):

$$\hat{X}_1 = 11.49 + .79X_2 + 2.25D_1 + 3.48D_2 \qquad R^2 = .29$$

$$\hat{X}_2 = -.22 + .03X_1 + .20D_1 + .30D_2 \qquad R^2 = .12$$

$$\hat{D}_1 = -.18 + .06X_1 + .13X_2 - .80D_2 \qquad R^2 = .45 \qquad [7.11]$$

$$\hat{D}_2 = -.39 + .06X_1 + .13X_2 - .56D_1 \qquad R^2 = .53$$

where X_1 is Parents' Education; X_2 is Community Type; D_1 and D_2 are dummy variables for Student Motivation; all variables are measured as before; and the R^2 is from predicting one independent variable, X_j, from all the other X_i ($i \neq j$).

These above equations are *not* explanatory. Rather, they are utilitarian, assessing the level of collinearity in the system according to the highest R^2 among the set. (Some statistical packages routinely provide a "tolerance" estimate with the multiple regression output, usually under a column heading of that name. In that case, $R^2_{X_j} = 1 -$ tolerance.) The highest is the last, $R^2 = .53$, a number far from 1.0, which would indicate perfect collinearity. This $R^2_{X_j}$ is well below that for the R^2_Y, the fit for the actual explanatory model (the R^2 for Equation 7.7 is .75). That is, one occasionally useful rule-of-thumb for signaling a high collinearity problem, that $R^2_{X_j} > R^2_Y$, is not violated. Overall, we conclude that the estimates from Equation 7.7 are not adversely affected by collinearity. More particularly, the non-significant results for the coefficients of D_1 and D_2 continue to stand. Simply because a coefficient is not significant, that is not sufficient ground for claiming a collinearity problem. Obviously, the discovery of lack of statistical significance may merely reveal that, after all, X is not likely related to Y. Conversely, *the presence of statistical significance indicates that, most probably, there is no collinearity problem.*

Suppose, contrary to the above example, that an analyst concludes high collinearity is a problem. What is to be done? The textbook solution is to increase the sample size, because that provides more information and may allow effects to be disentangled. Unfortunately, it is not likely that additional cases can be added. Usually, we are using all the observations we have! In that situation, alternatives become more difficult. Assuming, as we should, that the model contains the correct variables, then it is inappropriate to drop one or more out and present a revised model. Such willful specification error will guarantee biased estimates. A compromise position, which may serve, is to report two estimated models, the first with the full specification, the second with that specification minus the offending variable(s), as determined by the highest $R^2_{X_j}$. Perhaps—but this is only a perhaps—the substantive conclusions that the analyst reaches will remain the same, regardless. For example, it may be that the critical coefficient, say some b_k, is not significant in either model. (For more on the diagnosing of high collinearity, and other regression diagnostics, see Fox, 1991.)

Interaction Effects

So far, we have followed the conventional assumption, that the effect of one independent variable is the same, regardless of the value of another independent variable. That is, a unit change in X_1 can be expected to produce a b_1 change in Y, no matter the particular score on X_2, X_3, or X_k. Although this condition may frequently hold, it need not. When the effect of X_1 does depend on the value of X_2 (or some other independent variable), there is an *interaction effect*. If an interaction effect is specified for a regression model, it is incorporated with a multiplicative term, for example, X_1 times X_2, rather than the usual additive entry, for example, X_1 plus X_2.

Consider an interaction hypothesis for our Wintergreen College study. First, recall the benchmark of the original model reproduced below, where the effects are viewed as strictly additive:

$$\hat{Y} = 5.46 + 4.44 * X_1 + 11.28 * X_2$$

$$(.79) \quad (8.69) \quad (3.99) \qquad\qquad [7.12]$$

$$R^2 = .72 \quad N = 50 \quad SEE = 9.36$$

where variables and statistics are defined as before.

According to this model, students whose parents average an extra year of education can expect about 4½ extra test points, independent of whether they are from the country or the city. In other words, the effect of X_1 is assumed independent of the value of X_2. But is this a plausible assumption? Perhaps the effect of parents' education actually varies, depending on size of the student's home residence. One possibility is that parents' education transmits its impact less powerfully in an urban environment, because of competing socialization forces. Given such a circumstance, the slope of the Parents' Education variable is really lower for the urban students, as compared to the rural. That is to say, *the slope of X_1 should differ, according to the X_2 score*. To test this hypothesis, we incorporate the multiplicative term (X_1 times X_2) into our regression model, as follows:

$$Y = a + b_1 X_1 + b_2 X_2 + b_3 (X_1 X_2) + e \qquad [7.13]$$

and estimate with OLS,

$$Y = -.53 + 4.90 * X_1 + 34.75 * X_2 - 1.64(X_1 X_2) + e$$

$$(-.07) \quad (8.23) \quad (2.12) \qquad (-1.45) \qquad [7.14]$$

$$R^2 = .74 \qquad \text{Adj. } R^2 = .72 \qquad N = 50 \qquad \text{SEE} = 9.26$$

where variables and statistics are defined as before.

According to the interaction hypothesis, the coefficient b_3 should be positive and statistically significant but it is not. (The negative *t*-ratio of 1.45 falls well short of 2.00.)

Let us illustrate. Here is how the prediction equation simplifies for rural residents ($X_2 = 1$):

$$\hat{Y} = a + b_1 X_1 + b_2(1) + b_3 X_1(1)$$

$$= (a + b_2) + (b_1 + b_3) X_1$$

$$[7.15]$$

$$= (-.53 + 34.75) + (4.90 - 1.64) X_1$$

$$= 34.22 + 3.26 X_1$$

And, for urban residents ($X_2 = 0$):

$$\hat{Y} = a + b_1 X_1 + b_2(0) + b_3 X_1(0)$$

$$= a + b_1 X_1 \qquad\qquad [7.16]$$

$$= -.53 + 4.90 X_1 .$$

What we observe is that the slope estimate for urban residents is a bit greater than for rural residents (4.90 > 3.26), rather than the opposite, as hypothesized. However, more important, the difference between the two slopes (in the amount of 1.64, which is equal to b_3) is not statistically significant at .05.

In this particular research example, then, the interaction hypothesis fails to be supported, and we are left with the original strictly additive specification. However, generally speaking, with regard to the modeling of other processes, it may well be that interaction effects exist. If theory suggests their presence, the social science researcher should not hesitate to build them into a regression model. (For a detailed treatment of interaction effects in multiple regression, see Jaccard, Turrisi, & Wan, 1990.)

Nonlinearity

Until now, we have assumed that the dependent variable is a linear function of the independent variables. This assumption is more than a convenience. The accumulated experience of empirical social research demonstrates that, most of the time, it is difficult to improve on the linear specification. But there are clearly situations, theoretical and empirical, in which the linear model falls short. It is always necessary to think through the possibility of nonlinear relationships and explicitly model them if required. Fortunately, regression offers ample opportunity. The basic strategy is simple enough: If the relationship between, say, X and Y is nonlinear, a transformation is applied to linearize that relationship. After that transformation, OLS can be applied to the model without violating the linearity assumption. Below, we demonstrate.

In an earlier chapter, we began consideration of the form of the relationship between Parents' Education (X_1) and Academic Ability (Y). We assumed it was *linear*. In that situation, a unit change in X_1 produces the same

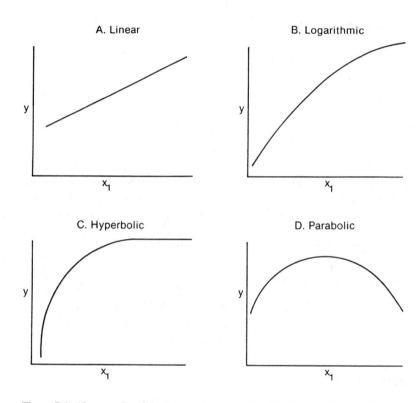

Figure 7.1. Alternate Possible Forms of the Relationship Between X_1 and Y

change in Y, *regardless of the value of X_1*. (For example, if the unit change occurs from 14 years to 15 years, it has the same impact as if it had occurred from 10 years to 11 years.) Theoretically, of course, there are other, nonlinear, possibilities. In Figure 7.1, we sketch three relationships, in addition to the baseline linear relationship (represented in Figure 7.1A). One such curvilinear possibility is that Y is a *logarithmic* function of X_1, of the kind shown in Figure 7.1B. Accordingly, a unit change in X_1 influences Y, but less and less as the value of X_1 increases. For example, an increase in education from 14 years to 15 years would have a positive impact on exam performance, but not as strong an impact as the change from 10 years to 11 years. Theoretically, this might be because extra years of high school are more important than extra years of college.

There are other such theoretical examples, where the impact of X_1 depends on its own value. A common one is where Y is a *hyperbolic* function of X_1, illustrated in Figure 7.1C. In that depiction, the impact of X_1, while always positive, diminishes rather quickly, eventually approaching zero. (For example, a unit change of education from 10 years to 11 years would have a relatively large influence, compared to a unit change from 14 years to 15 years. Moreover, a change from, say 19 years to 20 years would have hardly any impact at all.) Another possibility is a *parabolic* model for Y, such as that sketched in Figure 7.1D. Here increases in X_1 increase Y until a certain point, after which further X_1 increases actually decrease Y. For instance, it might be that positive changes in parents' education yield higher exam scores up to the postgraduate level (about 17 years of education), after which the increasingly high levels of parents' education somehow work to dampen their children's exam performance.

These four figures are represented mathematically in the following equations.

$$\text{Linear:} \qquad Y = a + b_1 X_1$$

$$\text{Logarithmic:} \quad Y = a + b_1 (\log X_1)$$

$$\text{Hyperbolic:} \quad Y = a - b_1 (1/X_1) \qquad\qquad [7.17]$$

$$\text{Parabolic:} \qquad Y = a + b_1 X_1 - b_2 X_1^2 \, .$$

The first model is the familiar linear relationship, between raw (observed) X_1 and Y. The next three models each "fit" the curved figures relating raw X_1 to Y, because of the transformation of X_1. (There is, respectively, a log, a reciprocal, and a square transformation of X_1.) Given that the particular nonlinear specification between raw X_1 and Y is correct, the appropriate transformation renders a linear relationship. For example, if the observed relationship between raw X_1 and Y is hyperbolic, then the observed relationship between the reciprocal transformation of X_1 (i.e., $1/X_1$) and Y will be linear. Thus OLS, with its assumption of linearity, may be correctly applied to the transformed equation.

Theory should guide the decision to model a relationship as linear or nonlinear. Sometimes, however, the guidance from theory is equivocal. We might argue that X_1 relates to Y in linear fashion. However, our critics may argue that theory dictates a nonlinear specification. Resolution of the debate receives aid from estimation of rival specifications. Suppose the debate is about our explanation of Academic Ability. We hold to our original linear specification, here labeled Model I. However, the critics, respectively, pump for Models II, III, or IV. (Note that all these specifications include variable X_2, Community Type, also considered by each as part of the explanation. It goes without saying that, in any model specification, some of the variables may enter transformed, some not.) Below are the OLS estimates for the four models.

Model I (includes no transformed X_1):

$$\hat{Y} = 5.46 + 4.44*X_1 + 11.28*X_2$$

$$(.79) \quad (8.69) \quad\quad (3.99) \quad\quad\quad\quad [7.18]$$

$$R^2 = .72 \quad \text{Adj. } R^2 = .71 \quad N = 50 \quad SEE = 9.36$$

Model II (includes natural log of X_1):

$$\hat{Y} = -91.31* + 60.77*(\log X_1) + 10.71*X_2$$

$$(-5.06) \quad (8.65) \quad\quad\quad (3.75) \quad\quad\quad [7.19]$$

$$R^2 = .72 \quad \text{Adj. } R^2 = .71 \quad N = 50 \quad SEE = 9.39$$

Model III (includes reciprocal of X_1):

$$\hat{Y} = 126.02* - 781.25*(1/X_1) + 10.43*X_2$$

$$(16.35) \quad (-8.27) \quad\quad\quad (3.53) \quad\quad\quad [7.20]$$

$$R^2 = .71 \quad \text{Adj. } R^2 = .69 \quad N = 50 \quad SEE = 9.65$$

Model IV (includes X_1^2):

$$\hat{Y} = -8.29 + 6.47X_1 - .07(X_1^2) + 10.98*X_2$$

$$(-.26) \quad (1.40) \quad (-.44) \quad (3.74) \qquad [7.21]$$

$$R^2 = .72 \quad \text{Adj. } R^2 = .71 \quad N = 50 \quad \text{SEE} = 9.44$$

where the variables and statistics are defined as before.

Review of these model results does not provide statistical support for a nonlinear specification over the linear specification of Model I. The *t*-ratios of Model I are larger, if only slightly so, than the *t*-ratios of the other models. Further, none of their R^2 are greater, and the SEE of Model I is lower, by a bit, than any of the others. Finally, the interpretation of the X_1 coefficient of Model I is general, pleasing, and straightforward. The same cannot be said of the X_1 coefficients of the other models. On empirical grounds, then, Model I seems favored. On theoretical grounds as well, it seems the strongest. Of course, for other social science research questions, a nonlinear specification might well carry the day, both theoretically and empirically. The analyst must always be ready to build nonlinearity into a model when theoretically appropriate, and to estimate it with OLS after proper transformation.

Summary and Conclusion

With multiple regression, we posit that a variable of interest, labeled Y, is explained by several independent variables, labeled $X_1, X_2, \ldots X_k$. Thus analysis begins with a theoretical construction—a model expressed in a linear additive equation. Estimates for the structural relationships are derived from application of ordinary least squares. The slope estimates purport to tell us what happens to Y, when X_1 or $X_2 \ldots$ or X_k changes, under controlled conditions. Are these estimates sound? The answer depends heavily on our diagnosis of assumptions and problems. Do we have the right variables in the model? Do they relate to the error term (which might represent omitted variables)? Are they measured at the proper level? Is there a problem of high collinearity? Should interaction effects be considered? Is a nonlinear specification preferred? When these issues indicate difficulties, we have offered counsel. As the reader has observed, OLS is

72

an extremely flexible tool, capable of handling almost all multivariate data analysis issues.

8. RECOMMENDATIONS

Curiosity about the workings of the world motivates data analysis. How did something happen? What are the facts of the case? Are they undergoing change? Why? In a statistical sense, a research question, even one of some moment, may involve the simplest of tools. Is the president unpopular with the public? How much has presidential popularity varied in the post-World War II period? These are issues of univariate statistics that might be tested with polling data. Does presidential popularity relate to the nation's unemployment rate? That is a question of correlation, its magnitude and significance. Is the popularity of the president explained by changes in unemployment, foreign policy, and racial tensions? The query has become more complicated and appears to lend itself to multiple regression analysis. Whether simple or complicated, such research questions can be intelligently addressed after careful reading of this monograph.

Still, we have not been able to cover, or even touch on, all the important methodological issues of quantitative research. The *complete* analyst will also have mastery of the literature on measurement, multiequation systems, and the relation between the two. Acquisition of all these statistical skills makes for a better researcher. Statistics provide a set of rules for social scientific discovery. However, the rules should never be followed slavishly. Judgment, insight, and serendipity play vital roles in the data analysis process. One valuable thought is worth a thousand computer runs.

9. APPENDIX:
THE REGRESSION ASSUMPTIONS

A failure to meet regression assumptions can mean the results we obtain are mere numbers on a computer printout. But, when the regression assumptions are fulfilled, the estimates from our sample data inform us of the structure of relationships in the real world. Technically, we then say that the least squares estimators are *unbiased.* (Suppose a slope is estimated over repeated samples, and the results averaged. If that average estimated slope equals the population slope, then it is unbiased.) With unbiased estimates, we are able to make strong inferences about the parameters of the population multiple regression equation.

$$Y = \alpha + \beta_1 X_1 + \ldots + \beta_k X_k + \epsilon. \qquad [9.1]$$

Some regression assumptions are implicit, some explicit, and different analysts may present them somewhat differently. (For an extensive treatment of regression assumptions, see Berry, 1993.) Below, they are listed briefly, with some annotation:

I. No Specification Error.
    A. Y is dependent (not independent).
    B. The independent variables, $X_1, \ldots X_k$, do in fact influence Y.
    C. The form of the relationship between Y and $(X_1, \ldots X_k)$ is linear (not nonlinear).

II. No Measurement Error.
    A. The variables are quantitative (not ordinal or nominal).
    B. The variables are measured accurately.

III. No Perfect Collinearity. (No independent variable can have $R^2 = 1.0$ when predicted from the other independent variables.)

IV. The Error Term ϵ Is Well-Behaved.
    A. It has a zero mean. (This assumption is basically relevant only for the intercept estimate.)
    B. It is homoskedastic. (Error variance is constant across the values of the independent variables. This is mostly a concern with cross-sectional data; for example, data gathered on individual units at one time-point.)
    C. It is not autocorrelated. (Error terms are not correlated with each other. This is mostly a concern with time-series data, where error at an earlier time, say $t - 1$, may be correlated with error at another time, say t.)
    D. It is not correlated with any of the independent variables. (This assumption is needed because we cannot experimentally control the independent variables.)
    E. It is normally distributed.

When assumptions I–IV.D. are met, least squares estimators are unbiased. The last assumption, IV.E., is not necessary for unbiasedness; however, it is commonly added to the list because it guarantees proper application of significance tests. (But even here, if the sample is large enough, the analyst may invoke the Central Limit Theorem and override the normality assumption.) Further, if the dependent variable is fully quantitative (i.e., not dichotomous and able, at least in principle, to take on a wide range of values), then assumptions I-IV.D. mean that the least squares estimators are also efficient. In sum, we would then say they are BLUE, for Best Linear Unbiased Estimator. (One estimator is more efficient than another if it shows less variance sample to sample. When least squares is the most efficient, it is therefore the "best.") If the dependent variable is dichotomous, least squares estimates are still unbiased but are no longer efficient, or "best." Thus an alternative estimator, such as probit or logit, which are more efficient, might be preferred over OLS (see Aldrich & Nelson, 1984; DeMaris, 1992).

REFERENCES

ALDRICH, J., and NELSON, F. (1984) *Linear Probability, Logit, and Probit Models.* Sage University Paper series on Quantitative Applications in the Social Sciences, 07-045. Beverly Hills, CA: Sage.

BERRY, W. D. (1993) *Understanding Regression Assumptions.* Sage University Paper series on Quantitative Applications in the Social Sciences, 07-092. Newbury Park, CA: Sage.

BERRY, W. D., and FELDMAN, S. (1985). *Multiple Regression in Practice.* Sage University Paper series on Quantitative Applications in the Social Sciences, 07-050. Beverly Hills, CA: Sage.

BOURQUE, L. B., and CLARK, V. A. (1992) *Processing Data: The Survey Example.* Sage University Paper series on Quantitative Applications in the Social Sciences, 07-085. Newbury Park, CA: Sage.

DEMARIS, A. (1992) *Logit Modeling: Practical Applications.* Sage University Paper series on Quantitative Applications in the Social Sciences, 07-086. Newbury Park, CA: Sage.

FOX, J. (1991) *Regression Diagnostics: An Introduction.* Sage University Paper series on Quantitative Applications in the Social Sciences, 07-079. Newbury Park, CA: Sage.

GIBBONS, J. D. (1993) *Nonparametric Measures of Association.* Sage University Paper series on Quantitative Applications in the Social Sciences, 07-091. Newbury Park, CA: Sage.

HARDY, M. A. (1993) *Regression With Dummy Variables.* Sage University Paper series on Quantitative Applications in the Social Sciences, 07-093. Newbury Park, CA: Sage.

IVERSEN, G. R., and NORPOTH, H. (1987) *Analysis of Variance* (2nd Ed.). Sage University Paper series on Quantitative Applications in the Social Sciences, 07-001. Newbury Park, CA: Sage.

JACCARD, J., TURRISI, R., and WAN, C. K. (1990) *Interaction Effects in Multiple Regression.* Sage University Paper series on Quantitative Applications in the Social Sciences, 07-072. Newbury Park, CA: Sage.

KALTON, G. (1983) *Introduction to Survey Sampling.* Sage University Paper series on Quantitative Applications in the Social Sciences, 07-035. Beverly Hills, CA: Sage.

LEWIS-BECK, M. S. (1980) *Applied Regression: An Introduction.* Sage University Paper series on Quantitative Applications in the Social Sciences, 07-022. Beverly Hills, CA: Sage.

LIEBETRAU, A. M. (1983) *Measures of Association.* Sage University Paper series on Quantitative Applications in the Social Sciences, 07-032. Beverly Hills, CA: Sage.

MOHR, L. B. (1990) *Understanding Significance Testing.* Sage University Paper series on Quantitative Applications in the Social Sciences, 07-073. Newbury Park, CA: Sage.

WEISBERG, H. F. (1992) *Central Tendency and Variability.* Sage University Paper series on Quantitative Applications in the Social Sciences, 07-083. Newbury Park, CA: Sage.

ABOUT THE AUTHOR

MICHAEL S. LEWIS-BECK, Professor of Political Science at the University of Iowa, received his Ph.D. from the University of Michigan. Currently, he edits the Sage monograph series *Quantitative Applications in the Social Sciences* (QASS) and the Sage *International Handbook* series. Recently, he completed a term as editor of the *American Journal of Political Science.* Professor Lewis-Beck has authored or coauthored numerous articles and books, including *Applied Regression: An Introduction, New Tools for Social Scientists: Advances and Applications in Research Methods, Economics and Elections: The Major Western Democracies,* and *Forecasting Elections.* Besides Iowa, he has taught quantitative methods courses at the Inter-University Consortium for Political and Social Research (ICPSR) Summer Program (University of Michigan), The European Consortium for Political Research (ECPR) Summer Program (University of Essex, England), and the TARKI Summer School on Statistical Models (Budapest, Hungary). Also, Professor Lewis-Beck has held visiting appointments at the National Institute for Development Administration (Guatemala City, Guatemala), the Catholic University (Lima, Peru), and the University of Paris I (Sorbonne) in France.